BILL RODGERS AND PRISCILLA WELCH
ON
MASTERS RUNNING
AND RACING

BILL RODGERS AND PRISCILLA WELCH
ON
MASTERS RUNNING
AND RACING

Bill Rodgers and Priscilla Welch with Joe Henderson,
Senior Editor, *Runner's World* Magazine

Rodale Press, Emmaus, Pennsylvania

Editor's Note
Times are ever-changing in masters running. World, national and personal records fall quickly and regularly. Marks listed here were current when the authors submitted final manuscript in late 1990. Many of these records will have been broken by the time you read this book.

Printed in the United States of America on acid-free ∞, recycled paper ♻

Book Design: **Peter A. Chiarelli**
Cover Design: **Christopher R. Neyen**
Cover Photography: **Ed Landrock/Rodale Stock Images**
Copy Editor: **Patricia Boyd**

Library of Congress Cataloging-in-Publication Data

Rodgers, Bill, 1947-
   Bill Rodgers and Priscilla Welch on masters running and racing / Bill Rodgers, Priscilla Welch, with Joe Henderson.
   p.   cm.
ISBN 0–87857–972–9   hardcover
ISBN 0–87596–330–7   paperback
1. Marathon Running.   2. Marathon Running–Training.   3. Running.
4. Rodgers, Bill, 1947- 5. Welch, Priscilla. I. Welch, Priscilla.
II. Henderson, Joe, 1943-
GV1065.P56 1991
796.42′5-dc20   91-11263

Distributed in the book trade by St. Martin's Press

2   4   6   8   10 9   7   5   3   hardcover
2   4   6   8   10 9   7   5   3   1   paperback

To my brother, Charlie, a real King of the Roads.

Bill Rodgers

To my husband/coach, David, who through his perception has given me so much encouragement and support throughout.

Priscilla Welch

Contents

Chapter 12: Running Faster, Farther, Better

Chapter 13: Aiming to Win

Chapter 14: Conquering the 10-K

Chapter 15: The Half-Marathon Challenge

Chapter 16: Competing in the Classic

Chapter 17: Mastering the Mile

Chapter 18: Off the Beaten Path

Chapter 19: A New Age of Champions

Acknowledgments

No book is solely the work of the people whose names appear on the cover. There isn't room there or here to credit everyone who helped with this book, but we do wish to acknowledge the major contributors.

Notably, we thank writer Katy Williams for assisting us mightily with the information collecting; Ray Cave, Nancy Lawentman, Angela Miller, and Suzanne Dooley of IMG; and Debora Tkac, William LeGro, and Kathleen Becker of Rodale Press for conceiving the project and bringing it to life; Marty Post of *Runner's World;* Al Sheahen of *National Masters News;* and Basil and Linda Honikman of TACSTATS for providing and checking statistics.

Introduction

October 1, 1988: While the Seoul Olympics dominated the news, half a world away in Iowa two over-40 runners were making long-distance history. Bill Rodgers was the first man and Priscilla Welch the first woman to cross the finish line at the Heartland Hustle 10-K in Davenport. At 10 kilometers (6.2 miles), which Bill ran in 29:48 and Priscilla in 34:28, the race was supposedly too brief for marathoners, which they both were, to dominate.

Bill had won the Boston and New York City marathons four times each. Priscilla had taken the overall women's title at New York and set a marathon world record for her age group at London, both in 1987.

What made their Heartland race historic was that never before in a major U.S. road race had both overall titles gone to masters—runners 40 and older.

Bill was then less than three months away from his 41st birthday, and Priscilla was seven weeks shy of her 44th. Their victories sent a message to older runners: Aging doesn't have to mean losing.

Portugal's Carlos Lopes had broadcast this same message four years earlier at the 1984 Olympic Games, where at age 37 he claimed the marathon gold medal while setting an Olympic record, which still stands. A year later, he set a world record.

Surveys taken by *Runner's World* magazine have pegged the median age of competitive runners at nearly 40—and it's rising. To the burgeoning masters populace, Bill and Priscilla represent two types of hope. Runners like Bill who start racing in their youth can stay competitive much longer than anyone once thought possible. And those like Priscilla who start late can make up for lost time.

Bill's fellow New Englander Johnny Kelley is the prototype of the lasting class of runner. Kelley won the Boston Marathon in his twenties and again in his thirties, set age-group records into his fifties, and still races in his eighties. Similarly, Bill first won at Boston at age 27 and still wins races in his forties.

British-born Jack Foster, now a New Zealander, is the prototype of Priscilla's late-starting breed. He began running in his thirties and set a world masters marathon record at age 41 that stood for 16 years. Priscilla began to run in her midthirties and remains at or near her best in her midforties.

In this book, Bill and Priscilla advise fellow masters distance runners—or "veterans," as the over-40's are known internationally—on how to last indefinitely in racing and how to improve performances for as long as possible. As their co-writer, I act as a conduit for their advice and a commentator on it at the start of each chapter.

I'm of their vintage. Like Bill, I've run since high school and have grown up with the sport. And I've watched Priscilla and other older runners prove that they don't slow down with age nearly as quickly as once believed.

The three of us often appear, together or separately, at prerace clinics throughout the country. Looking into those audiences, we see reflections of ourselves. The typical age is about the same as ours. The faces show the same mileage lines.

Yet the questions from audiences reflect a youthful outlook. The old-but-still-young runners are mildly curious to know how their heroes Bill Rodgers and Priscilla Welch got to be what they are.

But these runners don't attend these talks primarily to hero-worship. They're concerned with helping themselves. They come to learn, to overcome their own problems, to become better racers. Like the young, they still look ahead excitedly, seeing new possibilities and untapped potential.

They mainly ask us, "How can I run farther?" and, "How can I run faster?" and, "How can I stop getting hurt while running farther and faster?" Bill and Priscilla are, of course, elite athletes. But the answers they give to these questions apply to runners of all abilities.

At any level of ability and at any age, the runner wants to improve. If improvement doesn't show on the stopwatch, then at least it can appear as healthier and happier running.

This book is a printed version of Bill's and Priscilla's clinics. It touches lightly on their life stories without being truly autobiographical. They are more concerned here with helping *you* run and have the time of *your* life.

Joe Henderson

1965 Pre-running days: Smoking, drinking, and boredom was her military lifestyle.

1963 Bill set his first records in high school. "I quickly liked the idea of being successful."

1980 A year of ups and downs: Bill's fourth Boston Marathon victory and the U.S. boycott of the Olympics.

1986 "Being 40 and fast . . . gained attention quickly."

1990   "Athletes are saying, 'Why should I quit?' And I'm one of them."

1990   "My best racing is yet to come."

1

Starting Lines

Age Is Just One Number among Many

"Age is a myth." So said Priscilla Welch while celebrating her 43rd birthday two weeks early by winning the 1987 New York City Marathon. While starting work on this book at age 45, she still refused to concede that she had run her fastest times.

Meanwhile, Bill Rodgers had accepted the verdict of the calendar and stopwatch. He had slowed with age, no question about it. His times still looked incredible to other runners his age, nearly 42 as he started writing here, but he acknowledged that he was many years past his sub-2:10 marathons and near-28-minute 10-K's.

So, which runner do you believe? What degree of improvement can a masters runner expect? And when does the slowdown begin? In the separate and different stories of Priscilla and Bill lie two sets of answers.

Priscilla's Late and Fast Start

"Media interviews and question/answer periods after my clinics can be so boring these days," Priscilla said on the occasion of her 45th birthday, "because I'm always asked the same negative thing: 'When do you think you're going to slow down? When will your improvement stop?'

"Obviously, this will happen to me sometime. But it's a bad question that has no relevance to me at the moment, because I think there's still a heck of a lot of room for me to improve."

She wanted to tell doubters, "Look, I've heard enough of that question. Why don't you ask me when we're going to see a 2:25 marathon by a woman in her forties? Be more positive."

At this writing, Priscilla was thinking positively. "Now, a 2:20 or 2:23 is out the window for me," she conceded. "But 2:25 is still realistic. [Her best at the time was 2:26:51, the world masters record for women.] It just takes the right day and staying healthy for six months before."

Priscilla, along with Jack Foster and Carlos Lopes, appears to have broken some old rules. They all seem to have defied effects of aging that were thought to be "normal."

Conventional wisdom held that runners were supposed to peak in their late twenties and perhaps hold that edge into their early thirties. Runners a decade older weren't supposed to remain competitive with the youngsters.

Priscilla, who is from Britain, was 34 when she started running. At 39, she made the British Olympic team as a marathoner. At 42, she set her world masters record and won the overall women's title at New York City.

Jack Foster, from New Zealand, was 33 when he turned from serious bicycling to serious running. He set a world record for 20 miles at age 39. At 41, he placed second at the 1974 Commonwealth Games with the fastest marathon of his life—2:11:19, a time that lasted as a world masters record until the 1990 Boston Marathon.

Carlos Lopes, from Portugal, won a World Cross-Country Championship and an Olympic 10,000 medal at age 29. Then, injuries sidelined him for many years and almost ended his career. He came back at 37 to win the 1984 Olympic Marathon, and at 38 set a world record of 2:07:12.

Inspiring as these three stories may be, they don't belie the natural advantages of youth. They do, however, demonstrate that improvement is still possible after the supposed "peak" years have passed.

Priscilla Welch and Jack Foster sat out their "peak" years, and Carlos Lopes spent his injured. Had they been running then, their times might have been faster than the records they set in later years.

Cycles of Improvement

As it was, these three athletes proved that age isn't always as it appears on the calendar. Time spent running, the wear and tear of years of pounding pavement, may count more than chronological age. A runner's legs can be old at 25 or young at 40. Priscilla Welch and Jack Foster still had young, relatively unabused legs when they set their world masters records.

Foster had been running for about eight years when he ran his fastest marathon, and Priscilla's best time (as of this writing) came at the eight-year mark of her career. Their experience jibes with a theory that most runners can expect racing times to improve for seven to ten years.

Mike Tymn, a columnist for *Runner's World* and *National Masters News,* observes that many types of natural cycles are seven years long. Marriages, for instance, encounter the notorious "seven-year itch." Gail Sheehy's best-selling book *Passages* identifies major life changes at seven-year intervals. Workers are advised to change jobs every seven years. Farmers worry about swarms of locusts devouring their crops every seven years.

Tymn notes that a seven-year span of improvement is common among runners who race. Their legs don't suddenly fall off when this warranty expires, but performances do level off at about that point. He first observed this phenomenon in himself.

Tymn had run in his youth but returned to hard training and racing only in his late thirties. He improved until his midforties. Later, he noticed that his case wasn't unusual. Other runners' times often leveled off after seven years of racing.

Joan Ullyot, M.D., another *Runner's World* columnist and author of the book *Women's Running,* thinks the improvement cycle lasts a little longer—

Priscilla Welch, Year by Year

Here's how Priscilla Welch's times for the two most popular road racing distances have gone since she began running them in 1979 at age 34. She set her personal bests (indicated by *) in both the 10-K and marathon after her 40th birthday.

Age (Year)		10-K	Marathon
34	(1979)	42:42	3:26:12
35	(1980)	None	None
36	(1981)	None	2:59:43
37	(1982)	34:40	2:46:46
38	(1983)	None	2:32:31
39	(1984)	32:28	2:28:54
40	(1985)	32:14*	2:34:35
41	(1986)	33:08	2:31:14
42	(1987)	32:43	2:26:51*
43	(1988)	33:41	2:30:48
44	(1989)	33:08	2:35:00
45	(1990)	34:12	None

averaging about 10 years. One beauty of this 10-year period (and the 7-year period, too) is that the clock can stop in midcycle and then start again later with no time penalty, Dr. Ullyot says. Because of his injuries, Carlos Lopes required almost 20 years to put in his best 10. In 1988, Dr. Ullyot, then 48, improved a 12-year-old personal record in the marathon, but she had backed down to low-key running in many of her intervening years.

The greater beauty of the 10-year improvement clock, according to Dr. Ullyot, is that it doesn't begin ticking until the runner begins competing. So a 50-year-old novice racer is promised the same span of progress as a 15-year-old.

Ten years into her racing life, Priscilla Welch wasn't yet ready to say she had run her fastest times. She was out to disprove yet another old "rule," the one just outlined that says how long a runner can expect to continue to set personal records.

Bill's Long and Strong Career

A runner's prime years, said Bill Rodgers as he started writing this book, "relate not so much to age as to when you begin." His own running history supports the theory of a seven- to ten-year improvement cycle.

Bill's career began in earnest at 26. "I ran in high school and college," he said, "but I wasn't really a distance runner. The longest race was 5 miles in cross-country, and I ran 1 and 2 miles on the track."

He'd retired, apparently permanently, by age 22. Frank Shorter's Olympic Marathon victory several years later inspired Bill to begin racing again. "I won the 1975 Boston Marathon in American-record time of 2:09:55 at 27," Bill recalled. "Four years later, I set another American record — 2:09:28 — at Boston," which would remain his best time.

At 28 and again at 30, he ran 28:04 for 10,000 meters on the track. At 35, he PRed in the road 10-K with 28:16. "I didn't lose much by my midthirties," he said. "But since then, my times have started to fall off a little bit. I ran 28:55 as a 38-year-old, and my best time since turning 40 has been 29:48."

Facing Facts

This slowdown has caused Bill to face two facts on aging: (1) It may take ten years or so for the trend to appear, but everyone must slow down sometime, and (2) even if masters runners are still racing as fast as ever, they're probably recovering more slowly.

Jack Foster developed guidelines for dealing with both types of slowdown. Although he once competed on equal footing with marathoners a decade younger, they always held the advantage in recovery. And while he once averaged 5-minute miles in a marathon, he couldn't hold that pace indefinitely in the face of advancing age.

Showing wisdom befitting his age, Foster figured out sooner and better than most runners ever do just how long to back off after big efforts. His recovery formula has become a worthwhile practice for runners of all ages.

In a nutshell, the formula is this: Longer recovery time plus attitude adjustment plus realistic goals equals continued gratification and satisfaction with performance and achievement.

Taking Time to Recover

Even when he was racing his hardest and training his best, Foster took at least one easy day for every mile raced. This period totaled a week or more after a 10-K, and a month or so after a marathon.

He didn't completely stop running. But neither did he race again, or even train very long or fast, until the period of rebuilding had passed.

Bill Rodgers has trouble practicing such restraint. "Most years, I've run about 35 races," he said, "and I still average about 25."

Bill, however, acknowleged that his recovery time has slowed. He noted that "you can't recover as well at 40 or 41 as you did ten years before. You're not as resilient. You can't bounce back as quickly.

"When I was training my best in the late 1970s, I averaged 130 miles a week for three years. I can't do that anymore without risking injury."

His heavy racing schedule also puts him at risk. The day he turned 40, Bill injured an Achilles tendon. It forced him to drop out of his first marathon as a master.

Attitude Adjustment

Jack Foster's second trick is the harder one to master: adjusting to life after the last personal record is set.

The seven- to ten-year, or however long, period of improvement will some-day run out. It expired for Foster a long time ago. But he adjusted well to life after PRs.

In his late fifties, Foster races more than a minute per mile slower than he did at his best. But he speaks philosophically about the slowdown.

"The dropoff in racing performances with age manifests itself only on timekeepers' stopwatches," he says. "The running action, the breathing, and other experiences of racing all feel the same. Only the watch shows otherwise."

Bill Rodgers, Year by Year

Bill Rodgers has raced a marathon every year since 1973, and he recalls 10-K times for most of those years. These are his best marks through the years. ("t" indicates a track time; "c" is a 6-mile time converted to 10-K; * is his lifetime best; + is his best since turning 40.)

Age (Year)	10-K	Marathon
25 (1973)		2:23:12
26 (1974)	29:30tc	2:19:34
27 (1975)		2:09:55
28 (1976)	28:04t*	2:10:10
29 (1977)		2:10:55
30 (1978)	28:04t*	2:10:13
31 (1979)		2:09:28*
32 (1980)	28:43	2:12:12
33 (1981)	28:55	2:10:35
34 (1982)	28:26	2:12:39
35 (1983)	28:16	2:11:59
36 (1984)	28:53	2:13:31
37 (1985)	28:56	2:14:46
38 (1986)	28:55	2:13:36
39 (1987)		2:17:25
40 (1988)	29:48+	2:18:17+
41 (1989)	30:00	2:22:24
42 (1990)	30:08	2:20:46

Foster no longer compares his times with those from past races. He only compares his feelings.

Times change, feelings don't. Everyone's time will eventually slow down, but the effort and excitement of racing can remain constant throughout a runner's lifetime.

Veteran running writer Hal Higdon, who is Foster's age and has raced well for 40 years, says that "comparing this year's times, whether in training or races, with last year's becomes a downer. The obvious reason is the inevitable aging process that causes even great masters to slow down from year to year. By taking the emphasis off the clock, masters focus on their present rather than past achievements."

The Emotional Factor

If you don't look at the stopwatch, racing feels just like it always did. The anticipation and dread before the race, the strength and strain during the race, and the pride and relief after the race don't change.

Bill Rodgers has reached the Foster/Higdon stage of not mourning over his lost speed. But he hasn't reached the stage of not caring how fast he runs. He isn't looking back to break old PRs but looks ahead to breaking masters records.

"Running is not just about being fit and all the other reasons I like to run," he said at age 42. "I like to shoot for records of some type."

Those now are masters records. He set four such American marks—5-K, 8-K, 10-K, and 10-mile—the summer after turning 40, and more would follow.

"I want the American marathon and half-marathon records for masters [Barry Brown now holds them with 2:15:15 and 1:06:28], and maybe some track records," he said. "I still have these goals."

2

Priscilla's Eight Great Years

Her Journey from Beginner to World Class

May 10, 1987, was supposed to be Ingrid Kristiansen's day. The Norwegian was returning to the London Marathon for the first time since running her world best of 2:21:06 there two years earlier.

London again yielded a women's record, but it wasn't Kristiansen who set it. So much was expected from her, and she wanted so much from herself, that anything less than another world mark would mean she'd "failed." At 2:22:48, she indeed fell short, even though she won the race. This day belonged to the woman who finished second.

Priscilla Welch broke a world record, and a very durable one at that. Fellow Briton Joyce Smith, then 44, had set the masters best of 2:29:43 at the 1982 London Marathon. The 42-year-old Priscilla took almost 3 minutes off that mark.

Priscilla is the female counterpart of Jack Foster. She and the man from New Zealand both started running in their midthirties (unlike Joyce Smith, who'd grown up with the sport). Priscilla made the British Olympic team at 39, whereas Foster was an Olympian at 40. Both have held world records for their age groups.

Before Priscilla Welch, no woman over 40 had come close in the five years since Smith had made her mark. Priscilla's own 2:31:14 at Chicago in 1986 had been the nearest approach.

Priscilla ran 2:26:51 at London. And in the years since her triumph, no other woman master anywhere has ever broken 2:30.

Her record time carried many meanings:
* It buried the most venerable record in the masters record book.
* It bettered Priscilla's own personal best, set at the 1984 Los Angeles Olympics, by more than 2 minutes.
* It broke Veronique Marot's British all-age record by more than a minute. (Priscilla also beat Marot herself at London.)
* It placed Priscilla second in this race to the world's fastest woman of any age, Ingrid Kristiansen.
* It put Priscilla eighth on the all-time world marathon list for women of all ages.

Priscilla Welch couldn't have dreamed of coming this far, this fast, when she began running only eight years earlier. In her own words, she now traces her path from beginner, to Olympian, to world record-holder.

Pw From Military to Marathon

I had been in the Women's Royal Naval Service for nearly 17 years in 1979, and my last posting was to Norway. Thank goodness they sent me there!

The job wasn't all that satisfactory. I was really itching for something new to do and was already making inquiries about other work.

I was the supervisor in charge of a house rented by the British Navy for the WRNS—"wrens," as we called them. It was an additional job to the one I had been trained for, a secretary in the communications division. I had to make sure that the flag was flying properly and that we behaved ourselves and didn't embarrass our country.

I'd never had a job like that. I'd always been independent off-duty. I had a good bunch of girls, though, and we all got along like a good team. But to actually live in a house with all these people 24 hours a day was a bit much at times. So, to get away from them now and again, for release, and because I needed my privacy as well, I used to go for walks.

Meeting the Future

That's when I first saw David Welch, when he was out running. I never spoke to him then but thought, "He seems nice."

Then I met him in a bar. I'm a former smoker who'd given up that habit quite a while earlier, about 1970, but I still liked to drink sometimes. We got to talking in the bar. He told me he was in the military, too, working with supplies. He talked about his running and an upcoming competition he was entering. I must have shown interest, because he invited me along to watch.

Dave had always been involved in sports. He had just given up 25 years of rugby and had gone back to running. He'd competed in track as a youth. The first thing he did when he arrived in Norway was join a running club.

He took me to his club race, where I met up with a lot of his friends. I remember standing in the cold and rain, waiting for him to come over the finish line. Really, I didn't quite know what to do when he crossed the line.

I rather enjoyed the atmosphere at the races and loved the part of Norway I was in. Dave sort of opened up a new life for me. I had been getting a bit bored with the Navy because my social life wasn't very grand. There weren't many options for single folks attached to the NATO Forces in Norway, and I was also outgrowing my military career.

I eventually left the military but remained in Norway on a tourist visa, to be with Dave. But I didn't want Dave to finance me. I'd never had anybody look after me or pay my way before. Since I wanted to be independent but had no work permit, I cleaned houses during the 12 months it took for the permit to come through. I'd never cleaned houses before, and sometimes I felt miserable. It seemed such a comedown job compared with my military duties.

Dave felt sorry for me and started encouraging me to jog with Peggy, the wife of an American Marine major at the NATO base. That's when I stopped feeling miserable.

Starting Point

My first breakthrough came after three months of messing around with running. Dave tried to get me to run this all-women's race, a 10-K cross-country race just outside Oslo, and I resisted. I thought sport was for the younger person. Almost 35 then, I thought, "No way! I'm not going to make a fool of myself." But in the end, as usual, Dave's persuasion worked.

It was a warm day, and the course was a bit undulating. But I did 42 minutes and came in second. The much younger girl who won it was far ahead of me.

I was amazed at my finish because a lot of girls running in that race belonged to my running club, which had a lot of women who were very good cross-country skiers. Come skiing time, I was always way back. They didn't wait for me at all. I thought that cross-country skiing went hand-in-hand with running, and I just assumed that because they were good skiers they wouldn't have any problem with the run. I remember wondering where the hell they all were. Dave also couldn't believe I was second over the line.

That was a starting point. Dave must have realized I had some potential, because I wasn't even on a training schedule at that time. I was just pottering around on a daily basis, doing very short distances and gradually increasing when I could cope. As soon as I felt fine with, say, 2 or 3 miles, Dave encouraged me to run farther by adding an extra loop or two.

The First Marathons

We certainly weren't planning for a career in running. That sort of happened by accident. We were just running for fitness and health at club level. The more I did, the better I got.

David and I got married in October 1979, and after marriage I started working at the job I wanted, for a Norwegian oil firm. I was running to work at the time. We competed against other clubs, and I found this to be great fun.

I had run two marathons. The first was the inaugural Stockholm Marathon in 1979. We were going there on holiday, and Dave was going to run it. I sort of jumped in at the last minute. I hadn't been on a marathon training schedule, but I finished in the middle of the pack, with 3:26. Afterward, we went sightseeing and had to walk sideways down steps because we hadn't trained properly.

A month later, I did another marathon in Norway. I was still tired from racing a 30-K the week before, so my time was 2 minutes slower than in Stockholm. After the Norway marathon, I was so stiff and sore that I never wanted to run another marathon.

But in 1980, Dave heard about the first London Marathon, which would be run in 1981. He asked me, "Would you be interested in running that if you trained properly?" I didn't want to run any more marathons if they hurt as bad as the last one had. Stockholm had been fun, like anything you do for the first time. The second time wasn't so pleasant. When Dave said he would train me properly, I said yes, "provided this marathon won't be as painful as the last one."

We knew we had to take 12 months to train properly. So in 1980 he worked up a marathon schedule for the two of us. He researched it, went to meetings, spoke to people, read articles, and formulated his own opinions.

Only one of us could actually go to London, because we couldn't afford much travel then. Dave said I should go. He told me, "I think you can run within 3 hours, so you can better your previous time."

Sometimes, instead of catching the transport to work, I would run there with a pack on my back. Sometimes I would run on snow and ice, and people thought I was loony. Dave got me really tuned up for that marathon.

London: 1981

On race day in London, I took a train to the start. It was crowded with runners of all shapes and sizes, all talking about the race, and all excited.

We all got off at Greenwich and had to walk a spell—about a mile. Everyone was still chattering on about the race.

At the start, we were lined up according to time, with the slower runners farther back. I thought, "No, I want to get a bit closer." So I pushed my way up one or two blocks, to be nearer to the starting line. It seemed very, very crowded, and you had to fight to keep your position.

Before I knew where I was, I heard a big cannon blast. Then I thought, "This is it. This is what I've trained for. It's really happening!"

I had to walk three times in the last few miles. I wasn't aware of splits or anything. I was just out there to survive. During my last walk, I heard a voice in the crowd say, "Love, if you start running now, you can just get within 3 hours." Then I told myself, "Dave said I could run 3 hours. I had better do it for him." So I started running again and came over the line in 2:59-something.

I've never forgotten that first London race. It was really, really special. But I'd had to walk. I decided right then and there that I wouldn't walk at all in the next one.

The Only Thing to Do

After the race, I went back to Norway, and it wasn't long before Dave's new posting came through: the Shetland Islands. No one else would go there, and Dave agreed to go only after the Navy dangled a promotion in front of him.

When we arrived at Shetland, I was shown around the village. It took all of 15 minutes. I thought, "This is like the small environment I got away from at 16 to better myself." I'd grown up in the village of Upper Dean, Bedforshire (now Cambridgeshire), and until 16 had only traveled a small distance from home. The only type of work was on farms and in factories, and my parents didn't want me to do either. Shetland was similar but much farther north—more than 100 miles from Scotland's northernmost point—and the weather conditions were worse.

Dave and I looked at each other and said, "Oh, my, we've got two years here! How do we remain sane?"

The people up there worked hard, in oil, fishing, and farming. But their social life, drinking, wasn't our social life anymore. We'd done this in Norway, but I came to hate going in the bar and sitting and drinking until 1:00 A.M. To me, it became boring. Fortunately, we had the running as an outlet in Shetland.

Dave's idea was "Let's just keep our strength and stamina, and maintain our fitness for two years. Then we can start again when we go back to the British mainland." Little did we know that those two years would improve our performances tremendously.

At first, Shetlanders thought we were crazy. But eventually that wore off, because we were running all the time, every day, and everyone knew who we were and why we were out there. In fact, Dave started two running clubs — one of which remains active today.

We traveled down to Scotland to run races. We used to train for a marathon, save up for the trip, run the marathon, rest up, and then train, save up, run, rest up, and start all over again. We didn't have the money to fly to Scotland for 5-K's and 10-K's, so we just saved and trained and ran marathons.

International Breakthrough

In 1983, we returned to mainland Britain and settled in Cornwall. Dave was to leave the military shortly, but we soon learned that Cornwall didn't have jobs to his liking. A couple of moves later — in search of good jobs — we arrived in Kingston-on-Thames, near London, where Dave got a temporary job in a sports shop, selling running shoes. By this time, the autumn of 1983, my running had improved to quite a good standard.

We went to the 1983 Enschede Marathon in Holland, and I won the race in 2:36. That was my first real breakthrough as an international marathoner. I remember seeing all the British girls there parading around in their national track suits. They said, "If we're wearing these suits, you should, too." I did, and that was a big responsibility — wearing the uniform of my country.

We immediately started making plans to go to New York five weeks later. The previous year, we'd wanted to run the New York City Marathon but couldn't afford to go. This time, we called it a treat for Dave leaving the military.

Dave contacted Fred Lebow, the New York director, who gave a big no to our request for assistance with my expenses. But he did say, "If she does well, I'll pay her hotel and flight."

We found in one of the British running magazines an announcement of a tour to the New York Marathon. That's how we went.

Running in New York

Dave's instructions for the race were "Just enjoy it." It was raining that day, and the oil in the middle of the road was making my shoes slip and slide. My vision that day was only to beat all the British girls. Someone in the crowd mentioned the name of one of them, and the whole way I was looking for her and really gunning for her.

At 16 miles, I learned that I was in third place. I thought, "Well, I know who's in first: Grete Waitz. So the British girl must be in second."

er finishing third, I went to see who was second. It was Laura Fogli of *found* the British girl and asked, "Do you know I was gunning for you the *le* time?" She laughed and said I had passed her very early on.

That was my first case of playing a mental game, a first example of what you can put in your head during a race. I was looking for her, trying to get her, driving along, and I finished in 2:32, my best time to date.

So I got my flight money and hotel money. Fred Lebow had been true to his word. I also got some prize money, but I didn't know it right away. Dave asked, "Do you know what you just signed for?" When he told me how much it was, I went as white as a sheet. It was not a lot of money by today's standards, but it was the first real prize money I had earned.

"Not only that," said Dave, "do you realize you have the fastest women's British time this year?" And that led to another question: "Do we try for the 1984 Olympic Games in Los Angeles or not?"

Olympics-Bound

We decided to go for it. Dave quit his job to become my full-time trainer, and we contacted Nike to get contacts on where we could go to train. Thinking that my New York time might already have qualified me for the team, I talked with one of the selectors while on a training weekend with the British women's marathon squad. He told me that I was only on the "possible" list.

He said, "You've still got to run another race, the qualifying marathon in London, and see what the outcome is." So I did my best time of 2:30:06 in London, where I placed second to Ingrid Kristiansen of Norway, and of course was on the team. There was no question. The others were Joyce Smith and Sarah Rowell.

We had a wonderful team. Joyce was the old-timer and the fastest of us at age 46. I was the newcomer at 39. Sarah was a very talented youngster of 23.

The Payoff

Dave and I had first come to Boulder, Colorado, in July 1984 while training for the Games. Rich Castro, a local friend of visiting runners, had fixed us up with a flat, and we had a lovely time.

We chose Boulder because we wanted to try altitude training. But what was uppermost in our minds was getting used to the heat that we expected to encounter in Los Angeles. The only thing I found tough about the training in Boulder was the hot weather. Dave had me running around in sweats, and it paid off.

At the start of the Olympic Marathon, we saw a group of British spectators waving a flag. Joyce, Sarah, and I felt like a team, and we all hoped to place in the top ten.

The start was slow, and I remember thinking, "I'm still with them!" I just didn't know what I could do. Everyone let Joan Benoit Samuelson get away early, but I stayed in contention with the group behind her. I keyed off Grete Waitz, Rosa Mota, and Ingrid Kristiansen.

I crossed the line in sixth place with a British-record time of 2:28:54. I exploded with joy, like a 16-year-old gone bananas. Everything had gone well, I had broken the British record, and I was fresh as a daisy. Joyce was coming in like a train, and I ran across the javelin competition to shout her in. Then I ran across it again to yell Sarah in.

A woman official had to grab me and say that Joyce and Sarah could be disqualified if I continued. I came down to earth with a bang.

America Calling

After the Olympics, we went back to England but couldn't get settled there. Dave still couldn't find a job he wanted. And I'd turned 40.

A well-respected British coach, John Anderson, told Dave, "Take her to the States. She could do well. She's running a lot better than the 40-year-olds there. And apart from that, she'd gain a lot of experience there."

Dave agreed, but I was scared because we didn't have much money and I didn't want to get sick or foolishly injured. I didn't want to be broke in the United States, either. I wasn't prepared to gamble, because I had been brought up without much money and taught to be very cautious. It would be a big move for me. But Dave is more forward-thinking than I am, and very persuasive, so we went. We took our savings and planned to run until the money ran out, then come back to England and start over.

But we've never looked back. We came over on a six-month visa, went home, then were able to arrange longer visas because Dave could be a student at the Boulder School of Massage.

We chose Boulder, this time because we needed a base and were familiar with it from my Olympic training. Lorraine Moller, an Olympian from New Zealand who lived in Boulder, said we could rent a little flat from her.

Politics 1988

For various reasons, not the least of them politics, I didn't initially make the 1988 British Olympic team. I didn't take part in the qualifying race, which was

Priscilla Welch's Life and Times

1944 Born Priscilla Jane Mayes, November 22, in Upper Dean, Cambridgeshire, England, to Ethel and John Mayes.

1962 Joined Women's Royal Naval Service.

1979 Started running at age 34 while living in Norway . . . First race, a 42-minute 10-K . . . Ran 3:26 and 3:28 marathons . . . Married David Welch.

1981 Ran 2:59 in London Marathon . . . Moved to remote Shetland Islands . . . Won Glasgow Marathon in 2:55.

1982 Ran 2:53 at London Marathon . . . Repeated as Glasgow winner in 2:46.

1983 Returned to live in mainland Britain . . . Ran 2:36 and 2:32 marathons within five weeks, the former while winning at Enschede and the latter while placing third at New York City.

1984 Qualified for British Olympic team by running 2:30 in London Marathon . . . Finished sixth at Games with British record of 2:28:54 . . . Ranked eighth in world for year . . . Turned 40.

1985 Took residence in the U.S. . . . Set women's world masters 10-K road best of 32:14.

1986 Placed third at Pittsburgh (2:41:00) and Chicago (2:31:14) Marathons.

1987 Set world record for veteran women's marathon with 2:26:51 at London . . . Won overall women's title at New York City in 2:30:17 . . . Ranked sixth in world for year.

1988 Placed fourth at Boston Marathon in 2:30:48 . . . Won Heartland Hustle 10-K women's race outright.

1989 Masters winner at Boston (2:35) and New York City (2:36) Marathons . . . Won first ICI Masters Circuit 8-K championship race . . . Turned 45.

1990 Repeated as ICI 8-K winner in race-record time of 26:59 . . . Won masters titles at L'eggs 10-K and Bolder Boulder 10-K on the same weekend.

Best Times: (all after age 40 unless otherwise noted): track 5000, 16:13; 5-mile and 8-K, 26:17; 10-K, 32:14; 15-K, 49:35; 10-mile, 53:45 (53:51 as master); half-marathon, 1:11:03 (1:13:06 as master); 15-mile, 1:24:50; marathon, 2:26:51.

Height, 5'5½". Weight, 110 pounds.

the London Marathon. In any case, we had heard that the team would consist of the first two over the line at London and one other woman. We decided to take part in Boston instead.

I ran Boston with a stress fracture in my leg, although I didn't know it at the time. I couldn't train properly for the last five weeks. But I still ran 2:30:48 there, quite a good time for someone who hadn't done any quality work. I felt so happy that night, because I thought I must be on the team. The next morning, I was informed that I had not been selected. That decision was later overturned, however, and I did make the team—only to back out due to injuries.

Now, I'm aiming for selection in 1992. If my times are up there, I'd like to have another go at it. I expect qualifying for the 1992 team will be even more difficult than last time. I'll go to the qualifying race and do everything the right way. I want the hat trick, to be a three-time Olympian. I know this will be my last blast—my last shot at representing my country.

Age? What Age?

Had we come to the States and raced before I was 40, it would have taken a longer time to get a name and get known by race directors. Being 40 and fast was a good gimmick, because it gained attention quickly.

Yet I didn't take much notice of masters running then. I wondered what the big fuss was about. In my mind I was still competing in the open division, feeling no difference in age from the others.

I didn't think of age then, and I still don't give it too much thought—although because of the progress of the masters division and being such a standout example, I'm being forced to be more conscious of my age. But my age doesn't stop me from believing I can still get the training balance right and that my best racing is yet to come. ■

3

Bill Sets the Pace for Masters

Reflections on Running in an Age of Change

The baby boom was just beginning to roll through the country in 1947 when it spewed out a bumper crop of future elite runners. Forty years later, those now-mature runners were setting a fast pace for the future of masters distance running.

Jim Ryun was born in April 1947. He grew into perhaps the finest miler in American history and certainly the most prodigious, and was the last American man to hold a world record in the mile.

Ryun set that mark at age 20, placed second in the Olympic 1500 meters at 21, had his ups and downs the next few years, then retired from the track in his midtwenties.

Frank Shorter was born on Halloween 1947 in Munich, West Germany. He returned to his birthplace in 1972 to become the first American to win the Olympic Marathon in 64 years.

Shorter placed second in the 1976 Olympic Marathon in Montreal but ran faster than he had at Munich. His career has been on and off since then because of recurring injuries, several of them requiring surgery.

Bill Rodgers was born during the 1947 Christmas season. As a runner, he would be a slower starter than either Ryun or Shorter. Bill's career as a road racer hadn't yet begun when Ryun was a world record-holder and Shorter an Olympic champion. Bill never would succeed on quite as high a level, but he would prove to be more durable.

All three runners contributed to a great upsurge of masters interest in 1987, the year they turned 40. Promoters drew Jim Ryun out of track retirement (he'd continued to run on the roads) as a centerpiece for legends' miles at indoor and outdoor meets. Demand for Frank Shorter to appear at races, which had remained strong through the years, grew even stronger as he reached masterhood.

Both of them had lost some ground to the best masters, however, and were honored more for their past than present successes. Bill Rodgers was still succeeding. He had stayed as active as ever, and he always has been one of the busiest racers anywhere.

Rarely injured, Bill entered his forties still among the best American marathoners of any age. At 40, he led all U.S. finishers at the 1988 Boston Marathon. In his first few months as a master, he set world bests at four different distances.

His was the last and most-awaited of the 1947 birthdays. He would raise masters running to a new level.

Bill had nothing to do with organizing the first-of-its-kind ICI Masters Circuit in 1988. But his presence had much to do with its launching. He ran the first ICI race and many thereafter, including the series championship (which he and Priscilla Welch won). This guaranteed the circuit instant attention and credibility.

Masters running now had its perfect unofficial spokesman—one who best represented high performance combined with durability. Here, Bill reflects on who and what influenced him to become a master among masters.

BR "Why Quit?": Bill's Own Story

I've been lucky enough to spend my whole life in an area of the country with the deepest tradition for distance running. New England had great older runners long before the term "masters" was coined.

Frank Shorter, who attended Yale, and I are part of the deep New England tradition in long-distance racing. When Alberto Salazar, who grew up in the Boston area, broke my American marathon record in 1981, it really bummed me out for a while. But if the record had to go, I was glad it went to another New Englander. He took over the U.S. marathon lead from me. I'd taken it over from Frank. Before him, there were New Englanders Amby Burfoot (1968 Boston champion), John J. Kelley (1957 Boston champ), John A. Kelley (1935 and 1945 Boston winner), and the legendary Clarence DeMar (who won seven times at Boston).

Bill Rodgers's Life and Times

1947 Born William Henry Rodgers, December 23, to Kathryn and Charles Rodgers.

1963 Began running in high school at Newington, Connecticut.

1966 to mid-1970 Ran track and cross-country at Wesleyan University.

Mid-1970 to late 1971 "Retired" from running.

1972 Resumed training while doing alternative service as a conscientious objector at a Boston hospital.

1973 Ran first marathon at Boston, but didn't finish.

1974 Placed 14th at Boston Marathon with 2:19:34.

1975 Married first wife, Ellen Lalone . . . Was bronze medalist at World Cross-Country Championships . . . Won Boston Marathon in American record of 2:09:55 . . . Won Falmouth Road Race.

1976 Placed second to Frank Shorter in U.S. Olympic Marathon Trial with 2:11:58 . . . Finished 40th at the Montreal Games . . . Placed fourth in Olympic Trials 10,000 with PR of 28:04 . . . Won his first New York City Marathon . . . Ranked sixth in world.

1977 Won his second New York City Marathon . . . Won Fukuoka Marathon . . . Dropped out of Boston . . . Ranked first in world.

1978 Started Bill Rodgers clothing business . . . Won his third New York City Marathon and second Boston . . . Ranked second in world . . . Tied track 10,000 PR of 28:04.

1979 Won his third Boston Marathon in American record of 2:09:28 . . . Won his fourth New York City Marathon . . . Ranked first in world . . . Set world 25-K track record of 1:14:12.

1980 Skipped Olympic Trials after U.S. boycott announced . . . Won his fourth Boston Marathon . . . Published first book, *Marathoning*, coau-

One of my favorite running books is Clarence DeMar's autobiography, *The Marathon.* When I lived in Melrose, Massachusetts, I used to train on an old cinder track named for him.

A Slow Start

Not until I was in my thirties did I realize that DeMar had won his seventh and last Boston Marathon when he was 41. That was way back in 1930, decades before there were any special divisions for masters.

It took me quite a while to become aware of these legends. And compared

thored by Joe Concannon.

1981 Ranked seventh in world for year . . . Divorced from Ellen.

1982 Won Melbourne Marathon in 2:11:08 . . . Placed fourth at Boston.

1983 Married Gail Swain . . . Set road 10-K PR of 28:16 . . . Placed fourth at Boston Marathon . . . Won Orange Bowl Marathon.

1984 Finished eighth in Olympic Marathon Trial with 2:13:31 at age 36.

1985 First child, a daughter, Elise born.

1986 Placed fourth at Boston Marathon.

1987 Turned 40.

1988 Set world over-40 bests and U.S. masters records at 5-K (14:22), 8-K (23:51), 10-K (29:48), and 10-mile (49:24) . . . Won Heartland Hustle 10-K outright . . . Was first American finisher at Boston Marathon.

1989 Won first ICI Masters Circuit Championship 8-K race.

1990 Set world masters 10-mile record of 49:03 at Kutztown, Pennsylvania . . . Placed fifth (first American) in ICI Masters 8-K Championships . . . Fifth master (and top American) in Boston Marathon . . . Second daughter Erika born.

Best Times: Mile, 4:16; 2-mile, 8:53; 5-K, 14:22 as master; 8-K, 22:59 (23:51 as master); track 10,000, 28:04; road 10-K, 28:16 (29:48 as master); 15-K, 43:25; 10-mile, 46:35 (49:03 as master); 20-K, 58:15; half-marathon, 1:03:08; 25-K, 1:14:12; marathon, 2:09:28 (2:18:17 as master).

Height, 5'9". Weight, 128 pounds.

to what someone like Jim Ryun, who's my age, was doing at the time, I was a slow starter, a dabbler.

I used to run races with my friends when we were kids, just playing among ourselves, trying to find our way around in sports. We also enjoyed badminton and hockey.

Then I went out for cross-country in high school with my brother Charlie, and I really got caught up in it. We had a good coach, Frank O'Rourke, who's still at the same high school in Newington, Connecticut.

I had never done anything like cross-country before, and I happened to do it very well. That in itself was a great motivator. I quickly got to like the idea of being successful. In cross-country, I placed second in the Class A State Championships my senior year. In track, I finished third in the 2-mile. My best mile time was 4:28.

There had been no pressure at all to excel in high school running, and this approach continued at Wesleyan University, where sports had low priority and were strictly for fun. Academics were high-powered, and that was fine. Our coach was an ex-baseball player who gave us advice and monitored us, but kept things low-key.

Amby Burfoot was the star of our college team. He would win the 1968 Boston Marathon and later become the editor of *Runner's World.*

Jeff Galloway, a 1972 Olympian at 10,000 meters and now one of the leading running writers, also went to Wesleyan in the 1960s. So even though we had a low-key program, Wesleyan turned out some pretty good runners.

Frank Shorter went to nearby Yale, but he wasn't yet the great distance runner he would become later. Amby Burfoot beat him at the NCAA Cross-Country Championships.

In my first three years at Wesleyan, I was just a so-so runner. My best times had been a 4:18 mile and a 9:23 2-mile. In my senior year, though, I made a breakthrough with an 8:58 2-mile. Then I quit running.

Fall and Redemption

I finished school in December 1969. The Vietnam War made it a chaotic time—about 700 schools were on strike. I couldn't think about running in those circumstances. I didn't go back to running until I was working as a low-paid conscientious objector at Peter Bent Bingham Hospital in Boston. By then, I'd been inactive for about a year and a half.

I didn't have a car during that period. When my motorcycle was stolen, I started taking the subway to work, and later began half-running, half-walking.

When I lost my conscientious objector job at the hospital, I had nothing, no assets. The economy was in recession, and when I was fired, I didn't know if I had fulfilled my obligation or not. The government couldn't find me another job, and I wasn't sure if I had to keep looking for one.

For about a year, I was without a job. Even the motorcycle had been bought with borrowed money. I had a lot of negative feelings, and felt at the bottom. I remember sitting in a bar in Provincetown, Massachusetts, drinking beer and thinking, "I don't want to be like this." I got sick of myself, and that became my motivation to begin running again.

The only positive thing I could do was run. Running had always been something that I could do well and could come back to. Running was always there to pull me through, because it was under my control. It was purely a matter of focus, energy, and determination. I liked how it had always been a clear-cut avenue to success for me. Running was how I could redeem myself.

The Boom and I

The running boom had barely started when I began running again. Buddy Edelen (who set a world marathon record in 1963), Amby Burfoot, and Kenny Moore (who set an American marathon record in 1970) had been great American marathoners. But the media hadn't focused on them, so they were known only to other runners, and there weren't many of them.

Then came Frank Shorter's marathon victory at the Munich Olympics, and the sport suddenly exploded, both in terms of its number of participants and the attention it attracted. I was just starting to run again when this happened.

My career and the running boom have been very much intertwined. This has been true for the growth in number, size, and quality of races; the issues of politics and money; and the coming of age of masters competition. Just as I grew up with the running boom, I'm at the forefront of masters running today.

Into the Lead

The prime years of my career came between 1975 and 1980. That's when I won the Boston and New York City Marathons four times each, placed third at the World Cross-Country Championships, set a world record for 25 kilometers on the track, and came within one spot of making the Olympic 10,000 team.

In 1978, I won 18 races in a row. You've got those few years when you're at or near your best, and these were mine.

One of my greatest moments and one of my most disappointing moments came within a few months of each other in 1976. The Olympic Trial Marathon at Eugene, Oregon, was one of the most intense races of my life, and it was such an honor to finish within 8 seconds of Frank Shorter. Just making the team was a great thrill.

But it was very depressing to do so poorly at the Games in Montreal, placing only 40th. Compounding the disappointment was the U.S. boycott of the 1980 Olympics, when I was at or near my best. I felt crushed at the time, but it doesn't bother me much anymore. I moved on, looked ahead. I was still setting PRs in my midthirties, which the experts once thought wasn't possible. My marathon times stayed in the 2:13 to 2:15 range through the mid-1980s.

In 1986, when I was 38, I took fourth place at the Boston Marathon and beat one of the world's top road racers, Arturo Barrios. That showed me I could still have exceptional days. Physically, mentally, in every way, I still feel I have the capabilities to run 2:12 or 2:13 again. If—and this is a big "if"—I can stay injury-free.

The Age of Change

But it would be dishonest of me to say that age has taken no toll. I started noticing my slowdown at 37. My times in my late thirties were still pretty good compared to what 40-year-olds were running. At 38, I ran a 28:55 10-K, and that's 9 seconds faster than the current world over-40 road record. But because I placed only 16th in that race, my time got little notice.

Just two years later, staying free of injuries had become a problem for me. Through my whole submasters career, I never had a real injury. I never missed more than three days in a row while training between 1973 and 1987.

I beat Frank Shorter in my first masters race, but had Achilles trouble at the end of that 10-K race. Then I had to drop out of a marathon at Phoenix in January 1988.

But I recovered well enough to set over-40 world bests at four distances in my first year as a master, 1988: a 14:22 5-K at Little Rock, Arkansas, in July; a 49:24 10-mile at Flint, Michigan, in August; a 23:51 8-K at Indianapolis in September; and a 29:48 10-K at Davenport, Iowa, in October.

Yet I can't deny that my body has taken a lot of wear and tear, having been at it so long, raced so many times, traveled to so many races, and done so many promotions. I estimate that I've run 400 or more road races, and probably another 100 track and cross-country races in my career—most under 5 minutes a mile—and that I've run approximately 100,000 miles in training.

I can't push my training runs as hard. I can't do my intervals as fast. When I was 25, 28, even 33, I could shift gears in training runs. I could jump over logs. Now I have to run at a single pace. It's harder to train anaerobically. When I go to the track, my best workout is three times a mile in 4:35 to 4:37, with a quarter-mile jog. Ten years ago, I was going at least 10 seconds faster for those miles.

Paying the Piper

You must accept the changes. You can't tell yourself that you aren't aging. God made us this way. What I can do now is try to beat my peers. My only real interest in the marathon now is getting the American masters record. I hope it's still there for me.

But it'll be a tough record for me or any other American master to break. Barry Brown ran the best marathon of his life, a 2:15:15 at Twin Cities when he was 40. That's pretty unusual.

I don't think you can compare people like me or Grete Waitz (nine-time winner of the New York City Marathon) with masters runners such as John Campbell (world masters marathon record-holder) and Priscilla Welch. We've just been at it too long, while they've only been running for about ten years.

People have to understand the wear-and-tear factor. I don't think people who came along in their late thirties could run 50 or more marathons the way I have and still produce the spectacular times. John Campbell raced very well right after he turned 40, making the rest of us look terrible. But if he and I had been racing together 10 or 15 years ago, he wouldn't be running such fantastic times today.

The mistake we all seem to make is racing often and everywhere when we enter this new age group. There are only a few runners over age 40 who can train now as they did at 25. Careers are one part of that, and the wear-and-tear factor is another.

It's not only the older runners who slow down. Look at Alberto Salazar and Joan Benoit Samuelson, who both trained and raced very hard while in their twenties and have run into trouble. I wonder if they'll ever compete as masters. Frank Shorter also has been around a long time, and now he's paying for it with injury problems. Resting is the big issue here. People who hammer their bodies for years ultimately pay for it.

Shorter has the same lifestyle as I do, with all the same stresses of business problems, divorce, and kids. Not only that, but we have less energy to distribute over more areas. That's one reason we get injured more often now.

The Growth of Masters

When I started running road races, it was still odd to see older runners. It was nothing like today. An older runner like Johnny Kelley was the exception back then. He was a fixture at the races even then. At a clinic we held recently, we were asked how long we'd been running.

"A long time, nearly 25 years," I said. "Sixty-five years," Kelley answered. It boggles my mind to think that he has been running as long as my parents have lived.

Johnny Kelley is my Jim Thorpe. The rest of America may bow to the shrine of Thorpe, but to me Kelley is the greatest American athlete of all time. People always ask me if I'm going to do what Johnny Kelley has done. I just can't comprehend running that long. I do want to always be fit, and hope that it will always be through running. But I don't think I'll be doing the marathon my whole life.

When my running career took off, I realized that there was no good line of sportswear specifically for runners. Frank Shorter knew that, too, and started his own line of clothing after he took the silver medal in the 1976 Olympic Marathon. He even gave me an all-weather suit, but it was too small and I passed it on to Johnny Kelley.

I had already opened a retail store, the Bill Rodgers Running Center, along the Boston Marathon course. I saw no reason why I couldn't open my own sportswear company, too. Today it's called Bill Rodgers Sports Wear, and I still spend a lot of time doing promotions for my clothes.

I feel very lucky to have had my business career. But it hasn't been easy. Sometimes, running a business instead of running races has been a real drag. The business side is getting bigger and more important for me every year. I'll give up a training run to do a promotion because it's my livelihood.

Having my clothing line means I have to go to trade shows and race expos. I used to hate all that, but now I don't fight it as hard as I once did.

Maybe if I were semiretired from the business side of running, I'd stick with marathons. I know I'd get a lot of strength and energy back. I'll play this one by ear.

I know I can't compete with the best open runners anymore. But I try to beat as many of them as I can. My goal is always to try and win the masters division, or else do the best I can. Usually there are only three or four good masters in a race. But those three or four are some of the best masters in the world. The competition is there, and it will get more intense.

I don't think masters running has really taken off yet; it's still on the runway. The public is just beginning to notice us. Just wait until Grete Waitz, who turns 40 in 1993, and other well-known competitors race as masters. Someday we'll look like the senior golf tour.

We don't have that yet. We need more people, more names, and more competition. It's now like road running as a whole was in the 1970s and women's running was in the early 1980s, growing quickly. I think we'll see some good changes in masters running during the next few years. And I plan to play a part in them.

Athletes are now saying, "Why should I quit?" And I'm one of them. ■

4

Breaking the Age Barrier

Pioneers and Other Heroes in Masters Racing

Bill Rodgers was legendary among runners long before he turned 40. Priscilla Welch became a hero of all masters, women and men, soon after she turned 40. Bill and Priscilla now run amid thousands of hero-worshippers and legend-makers from their own generation.

Priscilla and Bill stand among the best-known runners in masters history. But they're far from the first of their breed. Runners competed at the highest levels long before their age-group became known as "masters." They raced and sometimes won against the best that youth had to offer.

A Long List

While laying the foundation for what was to follow, these pre-mass-movement masters labored in relative obscurity. Their efforts went little noticed and lightly rewarded. The list of historical figures in masters running is longer than one would expect, reaching back 60 years. If a Masters Hall of Fame were established, they would be its charter members. Bill and Priscilla credit three of these runners with influencing their own careers.

The Pioneers

Clarence DeMar won the 1930 Boston Marathon at age 41 and remains the race's oldest winner. He also ran in the 1928 Olympic Marathon just after turning 40, placing 27th, and still is one of only two U.S. masters runners to compete in the Games.

DeMar not only served as an early model for masters runners of a half-century later, he also enjoyed incredible durability, with his victories at Boston spanning 19 years.

The only other U.S. Olympic runner as a master was Johnny Kelley, another of Bill's heroes. Kelley made the Olympic Marathon team as a 40-year-old in 1948 and finished 21st. World War II probably kept him from being a four-time Olympian. (He'd run in 1936—the 1940 and 1944 Games were canceled.)

The war also interrupted but didn't end the careers of two older marathoners from Europe. Finland's Vaino Muinonen, 47, earned a silver medal at the 1946 European Championships Marathon. Britain's Jack Holden was 43 when he won both the 1950 Empire Games and the European Championships.

Seven Olympiads before Carlos Lopes' marathon victory at Los Angeles, Alain Mimoun gave preview to what a runner in his midthirties could do at the Games. The native North African, running for France, won the 1956 Olympic Marathon at age 35. Ten years later, he collected the last of his six French Marathon titles.

The First Masters

The first heroes of the first generation designated as "masters" were Jack Foster and Miki Gorman. Even now, they rank respectively as the world's second-fastest marathon man over 40 and America's fastest masters woman.

Priscilla Welch's first running hero, Joyce Smith, climbed to an even higher level of success, which no one topped before Priscilla. While both are British and have been masters marathon record-holders, the similarities end there.

Smith is a longtime runner. She ran the first 1500 meters at the Olympics (1972—she didn't reach the final) when that was the longest race for women. Twelve years later, she ran the Games' first marathon. She also won a World Cross-Country title in 1972.

Smith didn't gain international attention as a marathoner until she turned 40. She won overall at the 1979 Avon International Women's Marathon as a 41-year-old. At 42, in a 1982 race at London, she became only the fourth woman in history to break 2:30. At 46, she placed 11th in the Olympic Marathon.

The only masters woman marathoner now putting up Welch-like numbers is Evy Palm of Sweden, who is two years older than Priscilla. Palm, then 44, and countryman Kjell-Erik Stahl, 40, each won outright at the 1986 Stockholm Marathon. Palm repeated her Stockholm victory in 1987 and again in 1989, and ran her fastest marathon of 2:31:05 in London at age 47.

The Ultras

Note that the above stories all concern marathoners. The longer the race, the better the masters do. This may happen because the experience and endurance of age can outweigh the speed and strength of youth if the distance is long enough.

The past two decades of ultramarathon history also give ample evidence of masters' successes. In 1969, Ted Corbitt set an American all-age record of 13:33:06 for 100 miles. He was just shy of his 50th birthday at the time.

Between 1981 and 1984, Bernd Heinrich set American open records for 50 miles, 100 kilometers, 100 miles, and 24 hours. He ranged in age from 41 to 44 during that period.

At a major 100-K race in Minnesota during 1984, Sandra Kiddy pulled a triple coup. The 47-year-old beat all the women and men, and broke the American open women's record with 7:49:17.

Out of Africa

What might happen next in the age arena? Look for the East Africans to become the force in masters running that they already are in open road, track, and cross-country races.

Birth records weren't kept very carefully in this region before the 1950s, giving rise to some controversies over runners' ages. Ethiopian Mamo Wolde may have been 40 at the time of his bronze-medal marathon in the 1972 Olympics. Miruts Yifter of Ethiopia was anywhere from his late thirties to early forties when he won 5000- and 10,000-meter gold medals at the 1980 Moscow Olympics.

Kenya's Kip Koskei might have been as old as 41 when he placed third at the 1988 World Cross-Country Championships. Another Kenyan, Joseph Nzau, claimed to be 40 (but may have been as young as 38) when he ran well under the masters world mark, with a 28:09 10-K in 1989. That same year, documented 40-year-old Wilson Waigwa dropped the world masters mile best to 4:05.39.

Going Up

We're also about to see dramatically better times in the higher age groups. Joyce Smith turned 50 in 1987 and still competes, though with less seriousness than previously. Jack Foster, rather inactive in recent years, still could break age-group records in his late fifties and on into his sixties (which he reaches in 1992). At age 54 in 1984, marathoner Marion Irvine became the oldest qualifier in U.S. Olympic Trials history. She's now in her sixties.

Better and better times for older and older runners have been and continue to be the story of masters running. Talent spreads, both around the world and upward in age.

PW Priscilla on Joyce Smith, Evy Palm, and Women's Masters Status

Joyce Smith had a great influence on me, not because of her age but because of the type of person she is. I admired how she could train and race at such a high caliber, and still maintain the stability of her family as well. She has two daughters and got a lot of help and support from her husband, Brian.

She has been running for most of her life and still has the motivation to carry on. For many years, she was like a target for me. I wasn't comparing ages so much as I was aiming for her British record of 2:29:43. When I got it, at the Los Angeles Olympics, we posed for a team photograph with Sarah Rowell, the third member of the team.

I whispered in Joyce Smith's ear, "I'm sorry, but I think I've broken your record." I had just run 2:28:54.

She said, "Don't be sorry. You've earned it." She was very gracious, as I hope I'll be when my records are broken.

It was wonderful to be on the same Olympic team with her. She had been in the sport for so long and would soon be backing out of international competition yet was still able to train up to the required standard. I know she wants to break the 50-and-older record if she can stay free of injuries long enough to do one more marathon.

Today, I take inspiration from Evy Palm. She ran 2:31 at the 1989 London Marathon at age 47.

I think we inspire each other. Like Joyce Smith, Palm took part in the Olympic Marathon at age 46. And like Smith, she's a family lady. She has talent and trains hard, and I admire her for what she has achieved.

It gives me a bit of confidence to see there's somebody out there older than I am performing this well. I get bombarded with those questions about when I'm going to slow down, and I think, "Evy's 47 and just ran 2:31."

Evy Palm represents hope on the horizon. I look at her results and see that she's still motoring. If she can do that at 47, I'm hopeful that I can, too.

Room for Improvement

I wish there were more women like Evy Palm. But to be honest, the overall level of competition for masters women still isn't very high.

It has taken a while for the older women to build themselves up, both physically and in confidence. And not all of them want to get to reach a high standard. They're a bit scared. A lot of them are quite happy with their present levels. They don't think "open" (all ages running together), but only about winning the masters. You've got to think "open" to compete really well.

I think the ICI Masters Circuit is a good idea. It's not something I'm heavily involved in at the moment, because I'm still ambitious in open races. But I'm pleased to see there's money available for the other masters women.

What I don't agree with is paying a lot of money for a slow time. For instance, a 10-K time of 37 or 38 minutes should not be worth $1,000. Race directors need to rethink their prize-money setup and say, "Here's $1,000 for first place. But you have to run 35 minutes or better to earn it."

You've got to be fair to the open girls. In one race, I chose to compete in the open division, placed third, and earned $500. The top masters prize was also $500, for a time considerably slower, and that wasn't right. Maybe I shouldn't be saying this, because I still support masters totally. But I also want to see a stronger women's field all around.

Don't get me wrong. I like to see the masters earning a bit of money. But they should meet a certain standard in order to collect big money. There's improvement now among all masters, but it's slow. That's partly because masters competition doesn't come as easily for most women as it has for me.

I started running at almost 35, and I didn't have a family. My military career was ending. Many older women runners have been successful athletes for years, and many also have families and careers. They focus much of their energy on those activities.

Staying Hungry

When some women start running as masters, there's often something missing in their aggressiveness and hunger to go harder in their training and racing. They're reluctant to give up that much more time and energy.

They're used to bearing down for kids or jobs. But they're almost afraid to bear down with equal intensity in running, to go into it fully.

I know this a little bit myself, because I sometimes don't go full-out. I'm not obsessed with running. It hasn't taken over my life. I had a career in the military, but I chose to terminate it. And then I got married, which I never thought I'd do. Then I sort of drifted into another way of life, athletics, which is still all new and "Wow!"

But I know, because I'm 46 and have lived a bit, that there's more to life than running a world-record time or winning every race. It's not the be-all and end-all. I'm not obsessed with times or records. You ask me what my masters records are, and I can't tell you off the top of my head. I just go out and run the

(continued on page 34)

Masters Milestones

1930 American Clarence DeMar won his seventh Boston Marathon at age 41.

1936 Canadian Percival Wyer, still the oldest Olympic track and field competitor at 52½, ran marathon in Berlin Games.

1946 Finn Vaino Muinonen, 47, took silver medal in European Championships Marathon.

1948 John A. Kelley made his third U.S. Olympic team at age 40 and placed 21st at London Games.

1950 Briton Jack Holden, 43, won Empire Games and European Championship Marathons.

1966 Olympic champion Alain Mimoun won his sixth French Marathon title at age 45.

1968 Series of "masters miles" at open track meets in southern California led to formation of U.S. (later AAU, now TAC) Masters Championships . . . IGAL World Veterans Road Championships launched.

1969 Ted Corbitt, 49, lowered the all-age American 100-mile record to 13:33:06.

1970 Ted Corbitt set current American over-50 record of 5:35:03 for 50 miles.

1972 Ethiopian Mamo Wolde may have been 40 when he won bronze medal in Munich Olympic Marathon . . . France's Michel Bernard set over-40 record for 1500 of 3:52.0, which lasted 17 years.

1974 Jack Foster's 2:11:19 marathon.

1975 First World Veterans Championships held at Toronto.

1976 Japanese-American Miki Gorman ran first sub-2:40 marathon by over-40 woman while winning overall New York City women's title in 2:39:11 . . . France's Lucien Rault set current world over-40 track 10,000 record of 28:33.4.

1977 Miki Gorman, 41, won overall women's title at Boston Marathon.

1978 Britain's Joyce Smith set current world over-40 1500 record of 4:20.7 . . . Jack Foster became oldest sub-2:20 marathoner, with 2:17:29 at 46.

1979 Joyce Smith won overall at Avon International Women's Marathon . . . Clive Davies set current American over-60 marathon record of 2:42:44.

1980 Australian John Gilmour set current world over-60 track 10,000 record of 34:23.0 . . . Joyce Smith set world over-40 marathon record of 2:30:27 . . . Ethiopian Miruts Yifter may have been 40-plus when he won 5000 and 10,000 at Moscow Olympics.

1981 Joyce Smith's 2:29:57 was the first sub-2:30 for women over 40 . . . Mavis Lindgren set American over-70 marathon record of 4:34:08, which still stands . . . Bernd Heinrich, 41, set overall American 100-K record of 6:38:21.

1982 Joyce Smith lowered her world over-40 marathon record to

2:29:43 ... Jack Foster set current world over-50 marathon record of 2:20:28 ... A 2:13:41 marathon for Mexican Antonio Villanueva, 42 ... Bill Stewart ran 4:11.0 indoor mile, still a world over-40 indoor best.

1983 Sister Marion Irvine, 54, qualified for U.S. Olympic Marathon Trial with 2:51:01 ... American Doris Brown Heritage set current world over-40 mile record of 4:54.69 ... Mike Manley became first American sub-2:20 master marathoner, with 2:17:10 ... Bernd Heinrich, 43, set overall American 24-hour record of 156 miles, 1376 yards.

1984 Joyce Smith, 46, placed 11th in Olympic Marathon with 2:32:48 ... American Helen Dick set current world over-60 marathon record of 3:15:30 ... Barry Brown set current American over-40 marathon record of 2:15:15 ... Norm Green set current American over-50 marathon record of 2:25:51 ... Bernd Heinrich, 44, set overall American 100-mile record of 12:27:01 ... Sandra Kiddy, 47, beat all men and women of all ages in Minnesota 100-K.

1985 Priscilla Welch set current over-40 world best for road 10-K with 32:14.

1986 Sweden's Kjell-Erik Stahl came closest yet to Jack Foster's over-40 marathon record with 2:12:33 ... Stahl and Evy Palm, 44, both won overall at Stockholm Marathon.

1987 Priscilla Welch set current world over-40 marathon record of 2:26:51 ... Welch, 42, won overall women's title at New York City Marathon ... Evy Palm set current world over-40 track 10,000 record of 32:41.98 ... British-American Clive Davies set current world over-70 marathon best with 3:03:05 ... Ed Benham set current world over-80 marathon record with 3:43:27 ... Derek Turnbull set current world over-60 marathon record of 2:38:47.

1988 Bill Rodgers led all U.S. finishers at Boston Marathon ... ICI established circuit of masters road races in U.S. ... Kenyan Kip Koskei may have been 40-plus as bronze medalist at World Cross-Country Championships.

1989 World Veterans Championships in U.S. (Eugene) for first time ... Evy Palm, 47, won overall women's title at Stockholm Marathon after running PR of 2:31:05 at London ... New Zealander John Campbell set current over-40 world road 10-K best of 29:04 ... Australian John Gilmour set current world over-70 track 10,000 record of 38:27.0 ... Kenya's Wilson Waigwa set world over-40 mile record of 4:05.39 and 1500 mark of 3:49.47 ... Priscilla Welch and Bill Rodgers won titles in first ICI Championships.

1990 John Campbell broke Jack Foster's long-standing world masters marathon record, with 2:11:04 while placing fourth overall at Boston ... Bill Rodgers set world over-40 best of 49:03 for 10 miles ... Larry Almberg, 43, lowered American masters mile record to 4:06.70.

best I can on a particular day.

Maybe other women haven't got the confidence yet to go full-out. They're a little afraid to let go of the reins because of what it entails. I feel this in talking with women at running clinics. They ask David's advice on training. He tells them all that's involved, and they like listening to it. But listening and doing it are two different ball games. Maybe this will change soon, once they gain confidence.

The Thrill of the Chase

Grazielle Striuli of Italy, who beat me at the 1989 L'eggs 10-K in New York City, may signal a change for the better. She seems as ambitious as I am, and her husband is more ambitious than she is. He's really the driving force. He asked me how old I was when I had my best times. I felt like saying, "Well, I haven't had them yet." But you can't very well snap back like that.

I'd like to see other masters women like Striuli come along. The only American who's really aggressive is Laurie Binder, who also beat me in the Jacksonville River Run 15-K in 1989 when I was overtrained.

Maybe Binder is too aggressive. She's obsessed with beating my times. But I admire her for trying so hard while holding down a nursing career, which is very demanding.

The other women masters seem like an arm's length away. But one of these days, they're going to blossom. When this happens, I've got a feeling it won't be the old names who do it. It'll be new, hungry runners coming up.

In some ways, I'm glad that the improvement hasn't come any faster than it has. This has been good for me. But I don't know if I want to be winning so easily all the time. I like good competition. It's far more exciting and rewarding to be chasing someone than to be chased. The masters are chasing me at the moment, and they're having a hell of a time. It's exciting for them as they get a bit closer and closer, and eventually they'll go by me.

That's life. That's progress.

I don't believe there's one 40-year-old woman in the world who can always run faster than the others. I'm getting away with it at the moment, and that's nice. But it's also nice to strive for something. That's why I concentrate on the open division, because I'm chasing the little rabbits. That's what keeps me going.

And when they are too far ahead of me, there's going to be a lot of competition in the masters. Then I'll be running for my life in the masters. That's the way it should be. ■

BR Bill on Men's Masters Status

As Priscilla just suggested, the big-name runners in their late thirties today aren't automatically going to be the stars of tomorrow. Remember Carlos Lopes of Portugal?

People made him sort of an honorary master in 1984 when he won the World Cross-Country Championships, ran the second-fastest 10,000 in history, and took the Olympic Marathon gold medal—all at age 37. The next year, he repeated as cross-country champ and set his world marathon record. I saw him run a 28:56 10-K on the roads at 39, well below the current masters record.

We thought, "Wait until he turns 40. He'll blow all the records away." Lopes never thought about limits, yet he was aging like the rest of us. There has to be some slowing down. Something has to give. Injuries have kept Lopes from ever racing seriously as a master.

I remember Kjell-Erik Stahl of Sweden placing fourth in the marathon at the 1983 World Championships when he was 37. As a 40-year-old, he came the closest anyone had to Jack Foster's world masters record by running 2:12:33. We thought it might just be a matter of time until Stahl bettered Foster's 2:11:19. He ran many more fast marathons, but none approaching the record, and ended up developing a heart problem related to his diet.

Everybody takes a different path. Look at four-time Olympic gold medalist Lasse Viren, who's still running. Now that he's 40, maybe he'll put in a more severe effort. But I don't think the motivation is there for him anymore. He mainly wants to be fit now, and that's an admirable goal.

It shouldn't be held against Viren, Lopes, or Stahl if they don't race well now. They have already earned their medals.

So has John Walker of New Zealand, who won the 1976 Olympic 1500 and once held the world mile record. In his late thirties, he says he is retired from international competition. That's different from continuing to compete for a club or in road races locally, as Viren does. They can be great motivators for other runners in that way.

Herb Elliott, maybe the all-time greatest miler, still runs in Australia. Peter Snell, three-time Olympic gold medalist from New Zealand, still enters running events and triathlons. The great American miler Jim Ryun appears often at road races. I'm glad to see them staying very fit and competing without having to take it seriously.

Ron Hill from England, one of the top marathoners in history, is still at it in his early fifties. I can tell he loves to run, but he loves to travel even more. He has competed in 50 different countries.

Everyone has his own reasons for running, and these reasons can change through the years. Most masters are like other runners. They're not out to win races and break records every time. Only a fringe group is preoccupied with those things.

And it isn't always the names we've known a long time—the Shorters, the Virens, the Rodgerses—who are winning those races and setting those records. As I write, it's people like John Campbell and Priscilla Welch. Next year, it may be people whose names are still unknown today. ∎

5

Balancing Reversals with Renewals

What the Years Give to Performance, and What They Take Away

By George Sheehan's reckoning, Bill Rodgers and Priscilla Welch are still youngsters. Dr. Sheehan himself was in his athletic infancy in his forties, when he learned that he could be far more active in his next several decades than he'd been in his last few.

Dr. Sheehan had competed in high school and college track and cross-country, then had slipped into inactivity. He felt old at 45 when, as he describes it, "I pulled the emergency cord and ran out into the world. It was a decision that meant no less than a new life, a new course, a new destination. I was born again in my 45th year."

Long known as running's leading medical/philosophical commentator, Dr. Sheehan writes, "We are born with a 70-year warranty. But many people never bother to read the instructions. Three score and ten, the Bible promises us. But the average American newborn will never see it."

He celebrated his own 70th birthday by competing in a new age group at the 1989 World Veterans Track Championships.

Dr. Sheehan notes that "the instructions when we left Eden were simple enough: a six-day work week, and work that would bring sweat to our brow."

The hard work isn't required of most people anymore. But, says Dr. Sheehan, "The sweat of our brow, no longer necessary to earn our daily bread, has become even more necessary to make us fully functioning men and women. It now determines whether or not we will live a full 70 years, and live those years at our full physical potential."

We are not made, he says, "to break down, rust out, or come apart at an early age." When this happens, it is due to owner abuse and neglect, which the usual warranty doesn't cover.

Upkeep is the owner's responsibility. It involves putting out the right amount of physical effort and taking in the right amount and grade of fuel.

Most adults exercise too little and eat too much. "Too little exercise plus too much saturated fat, sugar, and salt cancel out the warranty," writes Dr. Sheehan. The result is an epidemic of early breaking down, rusting out, and falling apart.

Aging on Hold

The destruction starts from the inside—with heart and lungs that grow flabby, with blood vessels that get clogged, with blankets of fat under the skin. Go back to the original instructions, work up a daily sweat, eat lightly and naturally, and the breakdown can be stalled.

Distance running, when combined with a sensible diet, works the cardiovascular system, flushes out the plumbing, and eats away the fat. Running can truly keep a body young for its years.

Michael Pollock, Ph.D., has conducted extensive physical tests on champion athletes aged 40 and older. "It was particularly interesting to note the high maximum oxygen intake results," says the University of Florida exercise physiologist of the athletes' aerobic capacity. These runners used oxygen as efficiently as people less than half their age.

He adds, "Resting heart rate and body fat were much lower in the tested runners than in the sedentary population. Resting pulse rates were 10 to 20 beats below average for their age group. Body fat was about half the expected percentage."

However, cholesterol readings were below average only in athletes who carefully watched what they ate, Dr. Pollock says. "This agrees with other research findings that serum cholesterol appears to be affected more by diet than by exercise."

Even with continuing exercise, physical performance capacity naturally tends to drop gradually as we age, Dr. Pollock says. But scientists are also finding that long-time runners can slow the rate of decline dramatically. Even more amazing is the discovery that some older athletes can actually improve with age—*if* they learn how to adjust their training to compensate for the effects of aging.

Evidence grows that heart-pumping exercise such as running may add not only life to an athlete's years but years to one's life. Ralph Paffenbarger, M.D., an epidemiologist at Stanford University, is supplying such proof based on his long-term study of 50,000 men.

"The estimated additional life gained by adequate exercise, as contrasted with remaining sedentary, averages one to two years," says Dr. Paffenbarger, himself a marathoner in his sixties. "This significant difference is independent of other characteristics such as cigarette smoking, obesity, hypertension, or heredity."

Dr. Paffenbarger defines as "adequate" an activity that burns 2,000 calories a week—about 20 miles. "I think anyone could easily get to that level by spending a couple of hours a week running."

Dr. Sheehan adds that "running is part of ecology and preserving the good things. You're either growing up or stagnating. You can be old at 20."

Or you can feel young at twice that age, or more.

Slowing Down

Priscilla and Bill are perfect examples of the real and profound positive effects running can have on aging. It can delay or even reverse much of the decay we attribute to growing old—a decay that may in fact be the by-product of neglect. A qualifier, however, is needed here: Running does not suspend all the penalties of aging. A 50-year-old competes at a natural disadvantage against a 25-year-old.

As we pointed out in chapter 1, runners can reach their individual peak years at almost any point on the age scale. It all depends on when they start to run.

But the best of all runners generally peak within a rather narrow range of years, usually the midtwenties to the early thirties. Runners in this age group set most of the world and American records, because this is when physical speed and endurance combine with competitive opportunity and experience to best advantage.

Age-group record times fall off slowly but steadily from the thirties on up. The gap between the best times of older and younger runners is narrowing as more and better masters compete, but it will never close completely.

The overall world record-holders at distances of 1500 meters through the marathon average about 27 years of age, and none is older than 30. World records for the forties age group average 8 percent slower than the open marks. In the fifties, the gap widens to 19 percent. In the sixties, it reaches 36 percent. (The table on page 40 compares records for the age groups.)

Age Takes a Toll on Performance

Record times slow with age, as you can see by the tables below. We compared the open-age men's and women's world records with the fastest times in each ten-year age-group (through the end of 1990). Listed are the five most popular racing distances, the open record-holder's age, and the percentage of slowdown for age-group record-setters. For instance, the fastest man at age 70 runs nearly 50 percent slower than one in his midtwenties.

As masters participation increases, the quality of competition will improve, and the slowdown percentages will decrease. Note how much smaller the differences are for men than for comparably aged women, whose age-group program is newer and less developed.

Men

Event	Age of Record-Holder	Slowdown by Age-Group Record-Holder (%)				
		40–49	50–59	60–69	70–79	80–89
1500	24	10	17	29	48	74
Mile	24	8	19	29	51	78
5-K	26	6	16	28	51	69
10-K	25	5	18	28	43	64
Marathon	30	4	11	27	44	76
Averages	26	7	16	28	48	72

Women

Event	Age of Record-Holder	Slowdown by Age-Group Record-Holder (%)			
		40–49	50–59	60–69	70–79
1500	28	12	25	49	74
Mile	25	15	29	55	81
5-K	30	10	21	32	70
10-K	30	8	22	43	69
Marathon	29	3	19	39	94
Averages	28	10	23	44	78

The Test of Time

There are sound physiological reasons for this inevitable slowdown with age. Dr. Sheehan writes, "Alex Comfort, the world's reigning expert on old age, has proposed a battery of tests for the measurement of human aging. Its task: to pinpoint each person's status on the biological time clock.

"However, Comfort fails to list a short (less than 15-minute) test requiring a minimum of equipment (a stopwatch is the only essential) available to anyone over 40. It is called a mile run."

Dr. Sheehan notes that mile times show, more simply than any scientific test, the insurmountable differences in racing ability among the best runners from each decade. "A key to performance is the maximum pulse rate," he says. "This declines five to ten beats a decade, and separates the 30-year-olds from the 40-year-olds, the 40-year-olds from the 50-year-olds, and so on. This decrease in capacity for all-out effort amounts to a loss of at least 7 percent in performance per decade."

Dr. Sheehan himself once held the over-50 mile record at 4:47.8. He ran 22 seconds slower than the over-40 mark at the time, a gap of about 8 percent.

Dr. Sheehan quotes Scandinavian tests that indicate that a person's maximum heart rate at age 25 averages about 200 beats per minute. By age 40, it drops to 182 beats (a 9 percent loss), and goes down to 153 beats (down 23 percent from its peak) by age 65.

Maximum heart rate is a key to performance because it controls the oxygen that pumps through a racing body. The faster a runner goes, the more oxygen is needed. But the older one grows, the slower the heartbeat, so the less oxygen is available.

"No other determination or test," Dr. Sheehan concludes, "tells more about why we need separate age-group competition."

Age Is a State of Mind

Satchel Paige has something in common with Bill Rodgers and Priscilla Welch. Paige pitched major-league baseball somewhere between his late forties and early sixties. He either wasn't sure how old he was or wasn't telling.

Paige coined homespun philosophies that outlived his playing career. He's known best as the man who warned us not to look back, because someone may be gaining on us.

Once, when asked the inevitable question about his age, Paige answered with an intriguing question of his own: "How old would you be if you didn't know how old you were?"

Think about that. If you didn't know the year you were born, how old would you judge yourself to be? There is no more accurate test of true age than that. You can't tell by looking at your teeth, as you would with a horse, or by sawing yourself in half and counting the rings, as with a tree. You really are as old as you feel.

Age is what you make of it—a feeling that you're filling your allotted quota of years, or draining it. How old would you feel if you didn't know your age?

Larry Lewis of San Francisco, a runner and walker who worked as a waiter until a few months before his death at 106, never felt old. In fact, he hated that word.

"Never say a person is so many years *old*," Lewis once snapped at a reporter. "Old means dilapidated and something you eventually get rid of, like an old automobile or refrigerator. You're like a violin, a portrait, a wine. You mellow, but you never grow old."

Aging is not a death warrant. It's an opportunity to grow, to keep moving, to keep enjoying.

Aging has a plus side. With it come certain benefits:

• The pride of still performing well, even though you have put on more than a few miles.
• The wisdom that comes with experience, and the experience to use wisely what you know.
• The patience to let things happen at their own pace rather than trying to make them happen quickly.
• The confidence to go your own way, in your own way, at your own pace— without worrying about how other people do things or expect you to do them.
• The hardness that comes with absorbing decades of knocks, and the softness that comes with adjusting to change instead of fighting it.

The most admirable runners are those who last the longest, not those who race the fastest. This is, after all, an *endurance* sport. And what better measure of durability is there than running month after year after decade?

By that standard, Paul Reese of Auburn, California, ranks near the top. The retired Marine Corps colonel has run more than 200 marathons and ultras, plus hundreds of shorter races.

He has set age-group records into his seventies but says, "I don't want to leave the impression that I run and train for them. I've mellowed to the point where my singular goal is to keep running."

Reese has his priorities straight: "If I stumble on a record, fine. But, in the ultimate, I'd rather keep running another ten years recordless than stack up records over three or four years and then become runless."

Older runners come to know that the value of running itself is timeless and ageless. It is, in the words of Fritz Schreiber, who ran into his eighties, "a melody of my life, of all my life—to sweat out anger, to concentrate on the tasks of life, to feel the pleasure and delight of loneliness and freedom, to be all of a human being."

These values aren't measured on a stopwatch or on a calendar.

BR Bill on Aging

I agree 100 percent with Dr. Sheehan and researchers like Dr. Pollock and Dr. Paffenbarger. If you stay fit as you get older, if you continue to train steadily and consistently, and if you maintain pretty good flexibility and a good diet, you can slow down the aging process.

Athletes have always wanted to believe that. Now the researchers are putting the numbers together from large, long-term studies and coming to the same conclusion.

You also can make big reversals in your life even if you start running late, as Priscilla did. I really admire the people who decide to make these changes in their thirties, forties, or older.

An example is a man I met in Austin, Texas, as he was preparing to run a marathon. He was about 50 and an ex-smoker who had smoked for 25 years. For 10 of those years, he both ran *and* smoked.

He once lived a life where he didn't take care of his health at all. Then he took the first step—he started to do some running and changed his diet some. But he continued to smoke. Finally he took the *big* step—he started to take both his running and his health seriously.

My mother, Kathryn Rodgers, started running at 57 and now is in her late sixties. She has gradually changed her habits of exercise and diet.

She was always aware of what foods were good for her four children when we were growing up.

My mother was never really sedentary; she never sat around and ate chocolates. But she smoked for a while. Both of my parents did.

She worked hard taking care of the kids and the house, and that was her main occupation. She was sort of typical of her age group in that she didn't give herself much time to take care of herself physically.

But now, she has had time to learn about nutrition and cardiovascular fitness, and she's actively living the healthy life. She hasn't gone crazy about running, which pleases me. She doesn't call me up, asking for advice about training and racing.

Running is part of her life, but it's not an overwhelming part. Her main orientation is staying fit. She may not get out there every day, but she's well aware of the benefits of staying active—and the penalties of inactivity.

My father is the same way. He was a cigarette smoker, but he has changed his habits, too.

He was slightly overweight when we were kids. His motivation to get more fit was seeing the rest of the family doing it. His activities are now walking, jogging, and doing the yardwork.

According to statistics that I've read, only about 10 or 15 percent of Americans are doing what Mom and Dad do. That's a big problem in terms of our country's health and fitness, and a reason too many people grow old before their time.

One of the hardest things for young masters like me to do is find the time to run. Contrary to my image as someone who can spend all his time running, I'm busier than I've ever been in my life.

Before, there weren't as many activities to schedule. I could train more consistently.

The big difference for me in running now, even compared with five years ago, is all the demands that have thrown me off-track a little bit physically and psychologically: my family, my business, the promotions, the travel.

One of the changes in running over the last ten years is the increasing amount of work that runners like myself have to do for corporate sponsors. We're asked to do more and more for the same amount of appearance or prize money.

People call me up and ask, "Bill, can you come out to Los Angeles and do such-and-such?" Three days later, I'm gone. This makes my schedule very erratic.

Lots of times, I find myself really pooped and not able to train as much or race as well as I could. That's a big change between my forties and earlier years. I can't focus just on running, and I need to be more careful about how I ration my time and energy to make the running as good as it can be under these conditions. ■

Pw Priscilla on Aging

Let's look at the pluses of growing older along with the minuses. One plus is maturity. Masters generally can cope better mentally with longer-distance training runs and marathon races than younger runners can. Our recovery from hard efforts may not be quite as fast as it was before, but we compensate on the emotional side.

The younger person might prefer to run short and fast, and get bored with marathon training and the race distance. Our strength is our ability to concentrate and endure.

I'll admit that my recovery isn't quite what it used to be. My husband/coach Dave and I have adjusted my weekly program to allow for this. I used to schedule a heavy training day on Tuesday, a long run on Wednesday, and another quality workout on Thursday. Now I'm taking an easy day on Thursday and saving the quality work for Friday.

We found that schedule a lot easier for my body; three days of heavy training in a row was a bit much to ask of it. I think that even a young runner would find it hard to go for that third one.

The older you get, the more flexible you've got to be in your planning. I'm flexible in my training as long as it all works out right in the end, and in the end I do just as much hard work. As Dave says, "It's ridiculous to assume that a masters runner can become a world-class runner by training less than a younger runner. If a masters runner wants to compete at a world-class level, then she's got to train every bit as hard as the young ones do."

We're still playing with the question of concessions to age. It's a big mental game. So many people have been mentally conditioned to believe, "You can't do this at that age," or, "Don't you find it tough at this age?" It's all negative talk.

I don't know whether I've got my head buried in the sand or not. But I believe there's a lot you can get out of yourself at 45. Obviously, you do lose speed somewhere along the line. But I think that point comes later than most people now believe.

Too many people are stopping themselves from doing great things because they're "not supposed to" do them. I want to show them that they can go beyond these artificial limitations.

I could easily have settled for a life of limited vision. In my late twenties, I had left the military, didn't have many friends, and was mainly just going to and from work.

I remember thinking, "Gosh, if I've got to do this until I retire, it will be damned boring. There must be something else I can do with my life."

I was sharing a house with an older woman who said, "Well, you were once in the military and were very keen on that. Why don't you see if you can reenter? You'll have companionship, better pay and travel, and you can see where you go from there."

Eventually, I rejoined the military. But it wasn't until Dave came to Norway that all the good things that the woman had predicted started to come true. I had wanted to find something I was really interested in. The fitter I got through the training schedule that Dave had given me, the better I felt about myself and about life in general.

Running was making me a lot perkier, and a better person to live with. My exterior looks a bit worn now, but the inside feels very young. ∎

6

Learning to Run Smarter

The New Way to Train
without Injury

Down-time is a fact of most runners' lives. Surveys taken by *Runner's World* magazine indicate that nearly two-thirds of its readers will suffer medical problems serious enough to reduce or curtail training for at least one week of any year.

Bill Rodgers and Priscilla Welch aren't immune. As they will explain later in this chapter, both of them sometimes suffer along with the majority.

Most running injuries are self-inflicted, resulting from neither a competitor's blows nor random accidents. The stress of running itself is to blame in a high percentage of cases.

Certain viruses such as the common cold also can be self-inflicted. You're constantly exposed to these illnesses, yet they rarely surface unless stress has broken down your body's natural defenses.

Stress You Can Control

At the root of running injuries and illnesses lies stress. You improve by gradually adapting to the stresses of running, but break down by overdosing on these stresses.

The great majority of medical conditions that slow or stop runners grow out of too much work piled on a body not conditioned to handle such a load. In this fact lies hope. Because *you* cause most of your own ailments, *you* can also prevent them.

Prevention could be as simple as running very little. Kenneth Cooper, M.D., the man who coined the term "aerobic," reveals that training no more than 3 miles five days a week keeps the activity quite safe.

But runners who race won't settle for minimum requirements. To race farther and faster, they train harder—and thereby gamble with overstressing.

Masters racers face better odds of overstressing than younger athletes. Problems tend to surface more quickly and heal more slowly with age, and the stresses of life outside of running (mainly career and family) tend to grow.

All that you do, think, and feel affects how you run. Walt Schafer, Ph.D., a psychology researcher at Chico State University in California, says that emotional traumas leave a runner more exposed to apparently unrelated injury, and vice versa.

Dr. Schafer, a stress-management specialist as well as a competitive runner in his fifties, refers to a scale developed by two psychologists, Dr. Thomas Holmes and Dr. Richard Rahe, that measures the stresses of life events. These range from death of a spouse (100 points) and divorce (73 points) down to minor brushes with the law (11 points).

On the basis of their research with thousands of people from all walks of life, says Dr. Schafer, they found that the rate of serious illness rose along with the severity of stress in their lives.

Dr. Schafer has evidence indicating that the effects can be felt as injuries as well as illnesses. To test his theory, he questioned nearly 600 runners, using the Holmes-Rahe scale as a measure of stress. The key finding: The greater the stress over the past year, the greater the number of running injuries and days of running missed due to injuries during the past three months.

Dr. Schafer advises that whenever overall stress levels climb dangerously high for whatever reason—physical, emotional, social, or environmental—you should try to lower the stress factor over which you have the most control: your running program.

"Keep training during periods of high stress," he suggests, "but with moderation and sensitivity to early warning signs of injury and illness. Back off in speed and distance when needed."

A Lesson Learned the Hard Way

A masters runner we'll call Don had that lesson forced upon him. A long-time runner and professional fitness instructor, he had for years preached the need for leading a healthful life.

Yet he says now, "I feel like a minister who suddenly realizes his son is a juvenile delinquent."

Don explains, "I almost made 30 years of running without any serious problems. But after turning 40, I became more competitive in my running and won numerous age-group events. I collected more trophies and medals in the next few years than in my previous 25. My ego was on a continuous high."

He fell into a familiar trap, however. The more he won, the more he wanted to win—and the harder he worked to keep winning.

At the same time, he absorbed new job-related stresses. He exceeded his capacity to shoulder these burdens.

He says that "in a period of approximately 12 months, all sorts of tensions hit me. I didn't realize the full impact until the end of the year.

"In December, I came down with my first serious injury and was on the verge of a nervous breakdown. I developed numerous symptoms and spent many hours in doctors' offices trying to discover what was wrong."

Only later did Don realize that he had exhausted himself. By then, he already had found his cure. It began when he lowered his racing and training sights to the levels that had served him so well for 25 years.

On the job, this recovering workaholic now "delegates responsibility to other staff members. I work normal hours, never taking anything home to work on in the evening."

He adds, "I have learned that when the floodgates open, one should temper those stressors that are controllable. The others will drive you bananas if you don't. It is the total, cumulative effect of stress that is dangerous."

Your Early Warning System

Fortunately, your body usually doesn't ambush you. It gives warnings of impending trouble—subtle warnings at first that give you a chance to make adjustments and ward off serious problems. (See "Warning Signs of Trouble" on the opposite page for a list of common signals.)

Dick Brown, a physiologist from Eugene, Oregon, has a simplified list of telling symptoms. When he was a researcher for the now-defunct Athletics West, the most successful American track club in history, he devised a set of guidelines for distinguishing between training and straining.

"We've all heard the admonition, 'Listen to your body,'" he says. "But many runners don't know what messages to listen for, or how to respond to them. Our research showed that three indicators have the potential to serve as general guidance tools for most athletes. They are hours slept, morning pulse rate, and morning body weight."

Brown's advice for using these figures:
• Measure, record, and maintain a running average of your hours slept, morning pulse rate, and morning body weight. The hours slept should be as close an

estimate as possible of when you fell asleep until you woke up. The 1-minute morning pulse should be taken before getting out of bed. The morning body weight should be taken after voiding and prior to any food intake.

• Compare each day's data with your averages by asking: "Did I sleep 10 percent less than normal?" "Was my morning pulse 10 percent higher than normal?" "Did I weigh 3 percent less than normal?"

• If you get one yes answer, cut back your training load if you are having trouble during the day's workout. If you get two yes answers, have an easy workout that day. If you get three yes answers, your body is telling you it needs more recovery time and you should consider taking the day off. Promptly taking one day off may prevent taking lots of days off later.

Masters runners in particular need good, guilt-free reasons like these to ease up on training sometimes.

Warning Signs of Trouble

The trick in training is balancing stress loads: Run hard enough to build but not so hard that you tear down. It's easy to detect whether you're succeeding or failing if you know what to look for.

Improved performance without injury or illness indicates that you're adapting nicely. However, when the stress load grows too heavy—from either running or outside sources—you will develop certain mild symptoms.

The symptoms listed below are warnings that more serious trouble might develop if you don't take immediate preventive action. Develop a sensitive eye to these signals. By quickly interpreting and acting upon these symptoms, you can usually stop trouble at its source.

• Resting pulse rate significantly higher than normal when taken first thing in the morning
• Sudden, dramatic weight loss
• Difficulty falling asleep or staying asleep
• Sores in and around the mouth, and other skin eruptions
• Any symptom of a cold or the flu (sniffles, sore throat, or fever)
• Swollen, tender glands in the neck, groin, or underarms
• Labored breathing during the mild exertion of a training session
• Dizziness or nausea before, during, or after training
• Clumsiness—tripping or kicking yourself, for instance—during a run over rather smooth ground
• Any muscle, tendon, or joint pain or stiffness that remains after the first few minutes of running

More Isn't Always Better

Historically, runners have been extremists. Even Priscilla and Bill admit they've carried good training methods too far at some point in their careers, and hurt themselves in the process.

If some of something looks good, we reason, doing *only* that must be better. If so much of something is helpful, we assume *more* must increase its value.

The training pendulum has swung too far too often. In 1954, Roger Bannister broke a 4-minute mile by running no more than ten quarter-mile intervals two or three times a week. Soon afterward, runners everywhere were doing twice as many quarters, twice as often—and suffering for it.

In the 1960s, Arthur Lydiard supplied a cure for speed burnout. He sent his New Zealanders on long runs, totaling about 100 miles a week, during one period of the training cycle. Olympic titles and world records followed.

Runners everywhere tried to improve on Lydiard's system by doing nothing but road running, year-round. Too much distance burned them out as surely as excessive speed had done earlier.

If history teaches us nothing, it will be repeated. The pendulum will continue to swing between too long and too fast.

Fortunately, two of running's most influential writers and speakers are now promoting the middle ground. They combine the best of speed and distance work with the all-important time to recover.

George Sheehan is known by many titles: doctor, lecturer, columnist, and author. But before he held any of these, he was a racer. A long-time runner now in his seventies, Dr. Sheehan still races every chance he gets, and his moods still parallel his results.

In his late fifties, Dr. Sheehan's racing performances were slipping. He was then running almost daily, racing most weekends, and feeling weary most of the time. He was becoming a victim of the accepted belief that performance declines with age—until he started to train *smarter* instead of harder.

He added a rest day to his schedule, and his performances improved. He added a second day off and did better yet. A third day without running paid off even more.

Dr. Sheehan finally settled into a program of two long runs (much longer than he was able to do when training more often) and a race each week. This combination let him run the fastest marathon of his life at age 60.

Age is a key factor in this discussion. Racing times don't necessarily have to fall off as we grow older, but recovery time invariably takes longer. With the median age of road racers now standing at about 40, runners are becoming more aware of the value of rest days.

When Jeff Galloway turned 40, he was running only half the mileage he'd run as a 27-year-old Olympian—but he was still finding this work, on top of growing business and family obligations, hard to handle. Chronic fatigue hung over him.

As a master, Galloway went cold-turkey into half-time training. Every other week he switched from daily to every-other-day running.

The rest days allowed him to train harder on his work days and actually *increase* his weekly mileage, still feeling fresh. After the switch, his 10-K PR as a master dropped by more than half a minute.

The hardest training for most runners to adapt to is the easiest kind. The best way to ensure that it is easy enough may be to reserve some days for no running at all.

PW Priscilla on Overtraining

I've been through the bad times along with the good. I hope that the worst of them has taught me how to make the best better. The Olympic year of 1988 brought hard-won lessons to me on how to recognize the signs of physical distress. It was a very nasty time for me.

I had run a qualifying time to make the British team for the marathon in Seoul, but the selectors had decided they weren't going to name me to the team. They later reversed that decision, and I started training so hard that I really wore myself out.

I had sleepless nights and was irritable. I felt my whole personality changing. My husband and coach, Dave, didn't notice anything, or so he said. But I felt dirty inside.

All sorts of jealousies were coming out because Dave was working as a massage therapist and having good conversations with women clients. I felt I was only there to wash his clothes and cook his meals. I felt bombarded with work and didn't feel wanted or loved.

Those are all symptoms of overtraining. But of course I didn't back off. I didn't think I could, not with the Olympic Marathon to run.

In the end, I had no choice but to back off. My body said, "Whoa! If this lady isn't going to ease up voluntarily, I'm going to make her do it."

And that's exactly what happened. I developed stress fractures in the right foot first, and eventually I had them in both feet because I ignored the warnings and kept running.

Those injuries kept me from running in Seoul. They also taught me how important it is to recognize overtraining, and how to back off before you get badly injured, become really ill, or create serious problems in your private life.

Dave thinks there's no clear signal that tells you when it's okay to push harder. If you're feeling good, you just know it, so you go out and get the job done. But if you're feeling tired, pay attention. Fatigue is your body's way of telling you to lay off. "If you have a hard session to do and you don't feel good doing it," he says, "then bag it. Have an easy day, and come back strong the next day."

Dave sets out a program of quality workouts for me where he tells me to do 15 of this or 20 of that. But that's just a general guideline. He leaves the details up to me and how I'm feeling that day.

If I've reached a point where I can't run properly and I'm slowing down a lot, then I don't try to complete the scheduled session. I'm not getting anything more out of it. I just do as many miles or repetitions, or whatever, as I can. And maybe the next time, I'll feel better and do more.

You've got to have a feeling for what is happening in your body, but it's got to be a true feeling related directly to pain or fatigue. It can't just be an excuse to stop because you don't want to run anymore.

Along with overtraining, the other major cause of injuries is overracing. We try to plan my year carefully so that I don't overrace.

When we first came to the United States, I tended to race too much because I had to get a little visibility. How can you get an appearance fee or a good shoe-company contract if no one knows who you are?

So I overraced a little bit that first year or so. But since then, I have cut back to a more reasonable number. I do three or four races as a warmup for a spring marathon, and the same for a fall marathon. In between are two or three months that we call "fun time."

It's a time we don't take terribly seriously. The main season has always consisted of three or four races leading up to the marathon, with maybe a couple of local races to use as a training session.

I'm usually able to race well shortly after marathons, too. A week after the 1989 New York City Marathon, I ran a 5-mile race in San Antonio. It was just a fun thing to do. Then I did a local 10-K race a week later and won a turkey for Thanksgiving. It was a spur-of-the-moment decision, and I felt fine.

Dave and I disagree on the wisdom of racing so soon after a marathon. Now he can have the last word on this subject: "Priscilla promised me she would jog the races, but she ended up racing. I think that was kind of stupid. She gave in to the temptation to overrace, a common problem with top masters. There's a load of them out there who think they can go to every masters race and pick up prizes. They're running around the masters circuit like chickens with no heads.

"They're never going to improve by doing that. But maybe you can't say they're wrong, because maybe that's the way they want to enjoy their running careers. Maybe they see themselves as having only two or three great years, so they've got to do all they can while they can." ■

BR Bill on Overtraining

Ever since I was a high school sophomore, I've taken a long view of running. I may not have always thought about it, but I sensed it and lived it.

Only once did I stray from the viewpoint of a "lifer" in running. I quit after college, and maybe it took that quitting to experience how it felt not to be fit. My disgust with that feeling led me back into running to stay.

Most runners in their twenties and thirties don't think much about the long term. But in your forties, you think about it more and more. It becomes very apparent to a master that if you want to continue running indefinitely, you have to train and race more sensibly. That means taking a few more days off. It means not running so much on the really bad days of heat and humidity or cold and ice.

It's smart to make those adjustments. But it's not always easy to be smart. I still find myself making some of the same mistakes in my forties that I made in my twenties and thirties. Only now, the penalties are higher. Injuries come on quicker and are slower to heal.

It's very tricky to figure out how to adjust your racing and training after 40. I raced very heavily my first year after turning 40. I tried four marathons, and that was too many! I just can't do that anymore.

I'm intrigued by nationally ranked runner Barry Brown. He also raced a lot right after his 40th birthday. He set many American records, including the 2:15:15 marathon that I'd like to break. Brown told me in 1988 that he was retiring from marathons and would cut back his mileage from 140 to 120 miles a week. I'm amazed that he still insists on doing that much. He could be tremendously fit doing 80, 90, 100 miles a week. He could play with those figures for a while, instead of burying himself under heavy mileage.

In Brown's case I think the mileage has brought him great success. But it can't last forever. Training hard has its drawbacks. It will knock you down sooner or later because the risk is always there. The more you do, the more you risk.

A lot of muscular, tendon, and skeletal injuries come from overuse, from the wear and tear of the hard miles. A good example is a heel injury I suffered.

It's clear to me that this injury resulted from years and years of pounding and irritation that caused calcification at the back of my right heel. When pain flares up there, it slows me down a lot and I have to adjust my schedule accordingly. I cut back the miles and the pace until I can knock the injury out.

I've had a lot of experience with these kinds of minor injuries. I've always worked hard to nip them in the bud.

Older runners have to figure that they have qualities that differentiate them from the younger runner. Maybe they need to get a little more rest, or use an exercise bike instead of going out on a run every day. Older runners need to loosen the hip, butt, and leg muscles more. I think we really need to work on our stretching as we get older. Although I've always done a little stretching, I believe my injuries can be blamed in part on my lack of flexibility.

I was also running too much on asphalt and not enough on grass and dirt. Hard surfaces can hurt your feet. Since you lose mobility in joints, ligaments, and tendons as you get older, masters runners need to run on the dirt and grass, where the cushioning can help compensate for their loss of mobility.

Flexibility of mind is just as important as flexibility of body. As Priscilla says, you have to be willing to change a workout according to how you feel that day.

I always judge how I feel when I wake up, during the day, and when I go out for my warmup. If I'm really tired during a speed workout, I'll chuck the workout entirely, cut it back, or do it at reduced speed. You should be able to feel how fatigued you are during the workout. Your body will tell you when to back off.

I'm certainly not as committed to my long runs as I once was. Ten years ago, I'd run up to 2½ hours nearly every weekend. I trained for the marathon year-round. I don't know if that was very smart. Now, I'll do long runs only on weekends when I don't have races, and then only for the three months before a marathon. If I don't have a marathon coming up, I don't do a long run at all.

I also don't do many long runs in the summer months anymore. After the Boston Marathon in April, my longest run for several months is just 1½ hours.

My mileage totals now vary widely through the year. I may go down as low as 60 or 70 miles a week, and up to 100 to 120 while preparing for a marathon.

These amounts may still sound high to most masters. I run this much because I still want to stay competitive in the masters races. I aim to break some records, but I'm also taking more of a long view. When I'm not able to do as much running, I don't mind that. In fact, I kind of enjoy it.

I hope that this attitude will enable me to keep going for years and years. I want to run all my life, just the way Johnny Kelley does. Sometimes, I think about how Johnny, who's in his eighties, gets up at 5:30 or 6:00 A.M. and goes out for an hour run. Then he has breakfast and paints or has his day free.

I look forward to living like that in my retirement. ■

7

The Diet of Champions

Nutrition Advice to Keep You Running Smoothly

Like religion and politics, nutrition is a subject of much debate and little consensus. Bill and Priscilla, likewise, don't toe the same dietary line.

Bill's Appetite

Bill's alleged junk-food habits are legendary. In fact, they've been the subject of cover articles in national magazines.

Running's leading physiology researcher, David Costill, Ph.D., once invited Bill to his lab at Ball State University in Indiana for physiological studies. He learned much from hooking Rodgers up to sensors and wires in a battery of tests. But he learned even more from Bill's eating habits.

Dr. Costill was finishing his lunch when Bill arrived, so they talked while the doctor ate. Bill, normally the best of talkers, seemed preoccupied. Instead of looking at Dr. Costill, he stared at his dessert. Realizing that his research would go nowhere as long as they had this barrier between them, Dr. Costill finally said, "Would you like this piece of pie, Bill?"—and Bill virtually inhaled the pie before the doctor finished his question.

Stories like this, spread eagerly by the running magazines, gave rise to legends about Bill's appetite and food preferences. George Sheehan, M.D., once wrote in his *Runner's World* column, "Like many high-mileage runners, Rodgers is a junk-food junkie. Those elite runners will eat almost anything, but they lean toward cake and pie, candy and pastry, soft drinks and beer.

"Apparently, this is the diet that runners' instincts tell them is best. As their mileage increases, so does their need for quick-energy junk food."

Dr. Sheehan explained that "running affects the 'appestat.' This is the instinct that tells us what, when, and how much to eat. The thermostat-like system shuts down when we sit around too much, but exercise keeps it working."

Bill runs up to 120 miles a week, and at less than 130 pounds, he doesn't have a very large fuel tank. To keep his energy up, his appestat sometimes tells him to take a 2:00 A.M. snack of milk and cookies to power his morning run.

Priscilla's "Sins"

Youth forgives many physical sins — too little rest and sleep and too much of the wrong types of food and drink. In middle age, we pay more quickly and dearly for these sins.

For Priscilla, the greatest penalties come due when she lets down her dietary guard. So she watches quite closely what she eats.

Priscilla has told Diane Hawkins of *New York Running News* that she is "100 percent convinced that good nutrition goes hand-in-hand with good performance. You are what you put inside your body.

"This especially goes for people past 25. Not that people under 25 shouldn't watch their eating habits. It's just that poor nutrition hasn't caught up with them yet."

Ironically, "good" nutrition and her good intentions dragged down Priscilla's performances one year. In 1986, she had overdosed on nutritional supplements and was unable to breathe normally. "I found out, shortly before the Chicago Marathon, that I was literally poisoning myself with vitamins and minerals," she says. Once the problem was discovered, "it took me six months to rid my system of these toxins." That period of time ended with her record 2:26:51 marathon at London in 1987.

Meanwhile, Priscilla also eased away from her strict vegetarian diet of the previous two years. Diane Hawkins reports that on Thanksgiving Day 1985, Priscilla's husband, Dave, ate turkey and she didn't. He ran a better race that weekend and recovered more quickly.

They immediately started eating white poultry once a week. They've since added weekly portions of red meat or liver, along with eggs three times a week.

"I know people talk about cholesterol, and I am careful about it," says Priscilla. "But I believe athletes need to eat meat occasionally, to build up their iron stores."

She quickly adds, "We all have so much more to learn about nutrition, and how people react differently."

Finding what is right for her has meant rediscovering what she once had as a child. Essentially, Priscilla has returned to the eating habits of her youth in England. Diane Hawkins writes that "her mother built up a very good nutritional base for her and the rest of the family, serving fresh vegetables daily, along with fish or meat once a week when the fisherman or butcher called. In between, her mother made pasta."

Priscilla notes that "unlike children today, we had no soft drinks, and we were allowed sweets only once a week." This childhood training now leads her to practice the adage: All things in moderation, including moderation.

While carefully watching her diet most of the time, Priscilla still allows herself a "sin day" once a week. She says, "It's not a whole day of ice cream and chocolate bars. It's just having on that one day something I normally wouldn't eat.

"It's like a game. You're good for six days, and on the seventh day you get a treat."

What's Best for You?

In general, good nutrition serves only as a catalyst to good performance. It doesn't directly make you a better runner—only proper training will do that—but eating and drinking right gives you the health that allows you to train, which in turn lets you run better.

Nevertheless, certain types of dietary adjustments do produce direct, measurable, and sometimes dramatic effects on running performances.

Bill's and Priscilla's experiences illustrate that successful nutrition plans span a wide range of possibilities. But that doesn't mean that anything goes.

Everything we ingest serves one or more of the following purposes: energy production (providing fuel for work), growth (building and repairing the body), and control (regulating body processes). Carbohydrates and fats are energy-producers, proteins are body-builders, and vitamins, minerals, and water are regulators.

The News on Carbohydrates

Athletes rely on the complex carbohydrates, or "carbos," for their steady sources of energy. In fact, runners naturally gravitate toward a diet rich in carbos because their appetites demand them. Carbos are a preferred source of fuel because your body can break them down easily. They are then stored away in your muscles in the form of glycogen, ready to quickly supply energy.

Your body can store enough glycogen to supply your energy needs—that is, if you provide your body with enough carbohydrates to begin with. If you don't, as many runners have discovered, you can run out of fuel before you reach the finish line. At this point, your pace slows dramatically and you're forced to walk or even quit completely. This is so common a problem with athletes that it's been dubbed "hitting the wall."

But with some planning you can avoid "the wall." Training will, of course, improve your body's ability to store and utilize glycogen. But that's only half the answer. In fact, according to *Runner's World* nutrition columnist Liz Applegate, Ph.D., athletes who train heavily and skimp on daily carbohydrate intake can lose some of the benefits of hard training.

Plan a diet rich in grains, breads, fruit, potatoes, squash, and pasta to build up your store of glycogen and to prepare for your best performance. (See "Meal Planning" on the opposite page.)

The Problem with Fat

Take a careful look at your diet. How much fat do you consume daily? The American Heart Association recommends limiting your consumption of fat to 30 percent of total calories, but the typical American diet is still too high in fat. The extra fat you may be consuming not only can add an extra inch or two to your waist, but it also displaces the preferred carbohydrates you would otherwise consume.

Another argument against fat is that it is a poor fuel. Your body doesn't process fat as readily as carbos. Unlike carbos, which are stored in the muscles, fat is stored in fatty tissue and reduced to free fatty acids *before* the blood transports it to the working muscles.

To limit fat in your diet, avoid fried foods, whole milk and whole-milk dairy products, and high-fat meats such as luncheon meats. Instead, eat lean cuts of beef, low-fat milk and low-fat dairy products, and limited amounts of baked goods.

The Protein Factor

As we stated earlier, protein builds, repairs, and maintains muscles. It also fights off disease and controls the hormones that regulate your metabolism. In the past, nutritionists believed that athletes really didn't need extra protein in their diets. *Runner's World* magazine reports that one leading researcher, Peter Lemon, Ph.D., from Kent State University, has shown that the need for protein does in fact increase with exercise. Dr. Lemon studied two groups of athletes: one that followed a diet based on the Recommended Dietary Allowance (RDA) for protein, and another that consumed almost twice the RDA. The group that consumed only the RDA showed a loss of protein, while the group that consumed twice the RDA retained protein. Nevertheless, it's important not to go overboard on adding protein to your diet. Excess protein in your system can actually be stored as fat, and it can aggravate dehydration.

Protein should comprise only 10 percent of your diet. Any runner can meet his protein requirements by eating the right foods: lean meat, poultry, fish, milk, and beans.

Liquid Assets

Water is a valuable nutrient that often is overlooked. Runners, says Dr. Costill, often become "chronically dehydrated." He found that runners tend not to make up deficits from day to day and may have to remind themselves to take extra liquids. A runner can lose a quart—about 2 pounds of body weight— before noticing negative effects. But as the deficit rises beyond 3 or 4 pints during activity, the body temperature pushes toward a critical level—it first affects your performance, then your health.

Drinking immediately before, during, and after runs or races won't completely eliminate losses. But it can replace enough of the lost fluid and cool the body temperature to a point at which exercise is at least safe and productive.

Dr. Costill says that runners tend to let the sensation of thirst rule their drinking habits, and thirst sometimes fibs about true fluid needs. "In laboratory tests that required about 4 quarts of sweat loss," he says, "we found that thirst was temporarily satisfied by drinking as little as 1 pint of water."

Repeated heavy drains and inadequate replacement lead to chronic dehydration. Guard against this by checking your weight each day. If you drop more than 2 pounds from day to day, you're a quart low on fluids. Drink up!

Meal Planning

You are what you eat. But as a runner, you also are very often what you *don't* eat. Eating the wrong foods at the wrong times can lead to running miseries, and—in the long run—it can develop into fat.

Eating too much, too close to a race can affect you immediately. Arthur Lydiard, the prominent coach from New Zealand, observes that runners rarely "collapse from malnutrition" during a race. But runners do have problems of the opposite type: doubling over with side pains called "stitches," making "pitstops" along the way, or simply carrying an unpleasant sloshing and bloated feeling.

Keep in mind that *when* you eat is just as important as *what* you eat. Nutritionists believe that it's important to eat a high-carbohydrate meal (about 70 percent total calories from carbos) two or three nights before the event. At the same time, curtail your running so you don't deplete your glycogen store with training. The night before the event, you can be sure your glycogen store is full without eating a heavy meal.

On the morning of a race, your breakfast should still consist primarily of carbohydrates, but keep it very light to avoid feeling "overloaded" and to avoid an upset stomach. For a 10-K, some toast or an English muffin should be enough to restore the glycogen your body used while you slept. For an event that lasts longer than 90 minutes, you may want to try a breakfast that includes a bit of fruit, some skim-milk ricotta cheese, and marmalade spread on toast.

Eat lightly, if at all, in the last hours before running—and especially before racing. If you planned your meals to accommodate your racing—just as you plan your training—your body should be well prepared and well stocked with the glycogen you need to fuel your efforts.

The one basic pretraining or precompetition rule: Err on the side of too little rather than too much.

The Slimming Benefits of Running

As long as Priscilla and Bill average 15 miles a day, they don't need to worry much about gaining weight. In fact, they expend so many calories that they must maintain high consumption just to fuel their runs and to prevent their weights from falling too low.

Weight loss is related to distance, not speed. One mile burns about 100 calories, no matter how fast or slow you run.

Two researchers from the University of Victoria, British Columbia, found that the fat-burning effects don't just add up with distance: They *multiply*. Physiologists K. E. Chad and H. A. Wenger reported their findings in the *Canadian Journal of Sports Science*.

They measured oxygen consumption during and after exercise periods of varying lengths on a stationary bicycle. The subjects worked at 70 percent of their maximal oxygen consumption level, a comfortable effort.

As you'd expect, 1 hour of training consumed almost exactly twice as much oxygen as a half-hour's work. But the longer session gave even greater aftereffects.

The body doesn't instantly shut down after training, like a car with its ignition switched off. Metabolism stays up for hours after you stop running, continuing to burn fuel at a higher-than-normal rate. Dr. Chad and Dr. Wenger found this effect to multiply with the length of the session. Subjects after a 30-minute workout kept burning oxygen at a higher-than-resting rate for about 2 hours. The afterburn of a 60-minute session didn't just double but jumped by 350 percent to 7½ hours.

Dr. Chad and Dr. Wenger conclude that if your goal is weight control, then train longer. Their findings suggest that training a full hour, three days a week works better for this purpose than six half-hour efforts.

This study leaves some questions dangling: How much greater does this aftereffect become on runs well beyond an hour? How does running at more or less than 70 percent effort affect the afterburn? How much more recovery is needed between longer efforts if it takes so much time to come down from them?

Further research will have to answer these questions. But we already know that regularly scheduled fat-burning runs—slow but long—rank among the most active, pleasant, and effective ways for masters runners to "diet."

BR Bill on His Diet

My bad food habits really have been exaggerated. Junk foods aren't the majority of my diet.

I don't think I could have done the racing I've done over 15 years if I had had a really poor diet. I would have been injured more, or sick, or anemic.

I'm not a junk-food junkie, as the magazines claim. I'm just a cookie junkie. My daughter Elise loves them, too, and that's what we usually have for dessert.

I love to eat cookies, and I'm not going to stop. But we do try to buy those low in fat. Still, a bag doesn't stay around the house for more than two days.

Like a lot of people who run high mileage, I crave sugar. I like to eat foods that are really delicious—like fudge, hot fudge sundaes, and peanut brittle. But I don't eat those everyday. I don't go crazy and pig out on them.

When I was at my peak, I ate other desserts that were better for me. I loved bananas and knew they were good for me, so I made banana milkshakes with molasses.

A running magazine analyzed my diet several years ago, when I was running 150 miles a week. I was so hungry from training twice a day that I did do things like put mayonnaise on my pizza. My diet was high in fat and sugar, but that has changed over the last decade.

Sometimes I still eat too many sugary snacks. And when I'm served meals on airplanes, I occasionally choose the dinner that's not as good for me. If I'm offered lasagna or chicken, I'll take the lasagna. When I'm really hungry, I go for the one that tastes better.

When I started running, I was like most high school kids, that is, not very much aware of nutrition. But I think runners naturally gravitate toward complex carbohydrates. Today, I still love pizza, and I don't think that's a negative. I do so much training that my body needs the carbohydrates to keep me going.

(continued on page 64)

Fat Figures

How much you weigh isn't a very reliable measure of fitness. How much *fat* you carry tells you much more. The scales don't account for differences in frame size, but body fat percentages do.

Regardless of how chunky or lean an individual might look or what the scales might say, the ideal fat readings are generally listed as 12 to 15 percent for men and 18 to 22 percent for women. Top runners average about 5 percent leaner for each sex.

Body fat checks are made with calipers, in water tanks, or with higher-tech equipment. These tests aren't as readily available as the bathroom scales but are important enough for you to seek out. Check with your doctor, local college, or fitness center for these tests.

Armed with a professionally calculated fat percentage figure, you can then estimate your fat percentage at any other time just by checking your weight and doing some simple math. Here's how.

First, establish your lean body weight. This is what you would weigh with zero fat. Subtract your body fat percentage from 100 to figure your percentage of leanness. Then multiply this number by your weight on the day of the test. (For example, a 150-pound runner with 15 percent fat has a lean mass of 85 percent. The 150 times 0.85 equals a minimum lean body weight of 127.5 pounds.) That lean figure changes little in adults. Any fluctuations in weight, then, are probably fat-related.

Once you have established this baseline number, weigh yourself regularly and check it against the tables below.

Body Fat of 10 to 15 Percent

Lean Weight (lb.)	10%	11%	12%	13%	14%	15%
95	106	107	108	109	111	112
100	111	112	114	115	116	118
105	117	118	120	122	123	124
110	122	123	125	127	128	130
115	128	129	131	133	134	136
120	133	134	136	138	139	141
125	139	140	142	144	145	147
130	144	146	148	150	151	153
135	150	152	154	156	157	159
140	155	157	159	161	163	165
145	161	163	165	167	169	171
150	166	168	171	173	175	177
155	172	174	177	179	181	183
160	178	180	182	184	186	188
165	184	186	188	190	192	194
170	189	191	193	195	197	200
175	195	197	199	201	203	206

Body Fat of 16 to 21 Percent

Lean Weight (lb.)	16%	17%	18%	19%	20%	21%
95	113	115	116	118	119	121
100	119	120	122	124	125	127
105	125	126	128	130	132	134
110	131	132	134	136	138	140
115	137	138	140	142	144	146
120	143	144	146	148	150	152
125	149	151	153	155	157	158
130	155	157	159	161	163	165
135	161	163	165	167	169	171
140	167	169	171	173	175	177
145	173	175	177	180	182	184
150	179	181	183	186	188	190
155	185	187	189	192	194	196
160	191	193	195	198	200	202
165	197	199	201	204	207	209
170	203	205	207	210	213	215
175	209	211	213	216	219	222

Body Fat of 22 to 27 Percent

Lean Weight (lb.)	22%	23%	24%	25%	26%	27%
95	121	124	125	127	129	131
100	129	130	132	134	136	137
105	136	137	138	141	143	144
110	142	143	145	147	150	151
115	148	150	152	154	157	158
120	154	156	158	161	163	165
125	161	163	165	168	170	172
130	167	169	172	174	176	178
135	174	176	179	181	183	185
140	179	182	185	187	190	192
145	186	189	192	194	197	199
150	193	195	198	201	204	206
155	200	202	205	208	211	213
160	206	208	211	214	217	220
165	213	215	218	221	224	227
170	219	221	224	227	230	233
175	225	228	231	234	237	240

In high school, I used to skimp on lunch and try to save money by buying ice cream instead of a meal. But then at dinner I'd get a decent meal like macaroni and cheese. My brother Charlie and my best friend Jason Kehoe (who has been a store manager with Charlie for years now) used to cut out early on the long runs in high school and go eat cookies at a girlfriend's house. I didn't know at the time what they were doing, so I stayed with the long runs. I ran more than anyone else in the school, although today it doesn't seem like that much.

Back then, on the days we had track meets, the team would eat steak and dry toast. I never ate the meat, but I would have the toast with honey. Even now, I go through periods when I eat a lot of toast after I run. I must need it.

My wife, Gail, is very conscious of eating a healthy diet and not gaining too much weight. One reason is that overweight tends to run in her family. (And that's true for mine, too!)

Gail made a decision to eat less fat, and she has been very strong about sticking to that. She says she feels much better since making the change. Sometimes I go with her to the grocery store, and we talk about what we want to eat. Gail has a natural affinity for vegetables, and lots of them. She makes even more of an effort than I do to include them in our meals.

I also try to eat foods low in fat. I eat a lot of rice, beans, potatoes, cereal, and pasta. Although I don't eat as much meat as I once did, I'm not a vegetarian.

Some of my cravings go through cycles. When I'm in Phoenix for the winter and Boston during the summer, fruit tastes delicious. I also eat less and drink more in the heat.

I'm a bigger drinker than an eater. And I'm not talking about alcohol, although I like a cold beer and some of the liqueurs. I drink a lot of diet soda. I first tried it when I noticed Greg Meyer, the 1983 Boston Marathon champion, drinking it when he worked in our store, packing boxes. I thought it tasted just as good as the brands with sugar. I used to like all the flavors, but now I prefer only those with no caffeine. I also stock up on flavored mineral water.

I drink far more water now than I did ten years ago, because I'm more aware of how important it is to an athlete. Drinking enough water is something I have to concentrate on every day, because I know I'm dehydrated a lot.

Since I've run almost nonstop since high school, my weight never has changed much. The one time I quit running, I went up to 140 pounds—about 12 pounds above normal.

For a while, I just accepted that extra weight. Then finally, I physically started feeling pretty poorly. As soon as I began to run again, my weight went back down.

I don't feel guilty about my diet unless I'm not training. Wanting to run as well as I can for as long as I can is a great motivation for me to eat better. If I weren't running, I'd be gaining weight. ■

Pw Priscilla on Her Diet

I really haven't eased my eating habits too much, because I don't think they were so extreme to start with. I still allow myself that one "sin day" a week, and I allow myself the occasional cookie.

But just as I'm diligent in my training, I'm diligent in my eating. I do watch my diet because I'm older, and at my age the body takes its toll if you don't watch everything. The younger runners can get away with more.

I actually didn't give eating much thought when I was younger, if only because I had good grounding as a kid. My family wasn't well off, and we had to grow our own vegetables. Twice a week, we'd have a little bit of meat. Once a week, we bought fish from a man who came around in a van. My mother made the rest of the food. We had a lot of potatoes and gravy, and rice puddings for dessert.

Breakfasts would be oatmeal, in the winter especially, with a big dollop of jam in the middle. It filled the belly.

The only sinful thing I can recall having was too much animal fat, although we didn't know it was bad then. My habits were well ingrained when I was a child.

Now that I'm running, I'm putting in good fuel. Basically my diet is 60 or 65 percent carbohydrates, and the rest is protein and fats. We find that's a good recipe. A lot of people make the mistake of going with the nutrition fad of the moment. Dave and I were vegetarians for two years. But this didn't work for us. We just missed having our high-quality red meat two times a week.

Phil Maffetone, a kinesiologist in New York, helped me in 1986 when I wasn't running well. I had problems staying aerobic and burning fats. He analyzed my diet and found that I had a high toxicity level in my system from overdosing on vitamins.

I had started off with multivitamins and soon was using the individual vitamins. When the trouble arose, I was popping 15 vitamin pills a day. No wonder the dose was toxic! Phil had me change my diet, and for six months I did no anaerobic training at all. Now I'm back to the single multivitamins.

If I were back in my little village in England, I wouldn't have to even worry about taking vitamins. I know the earth there is not spoiled. But now I get my fruits and vegetables from the city, and who knows how long they've been lying around? So I back up the foods with a multivitamin.

I prefer home-cooked meals to restaurant meals, although Dave and I like to go out to eat about once a week when we're in Boulder. You don't know what type of fat a restaurant uses in its meals. Also, restaurant meals tend to come with horrific creams and sauces. They're delicious and hard to refuse. But I know I've got to be flexible, since I must eat in hotels and restaurants when I'm traveling for a race.

Several rules on eating and nutrition work for me, although rules are different for different people. One such rule is to read labels. If a label reads "hydrogenated fat," for instance, I put the item back on the shelf. Fat will only make you fatter.

I like to drink seven or eight glasses of water a day but don't drink water with my meal. I avoid sugar and anything with sucrose. I eat honey and use sea salt. Chewing food properly allows the enzymes in the mouth to begin to digest the cooked starches.

With dinner, I like to have a glass of wine as my beverage, but not every evening. I avoid coffee, but being English, I do like a good cup of tea and drink the herb teas.

I'm sinful sometimes with my tea, but a little bit of what you fancy does you good. I allow for some fun food. ■

8

Reprogramming the Prime Years

Tips for Setting Up a Beginner's Plan

Bill Rodgers never was a true beginning runner. He already was fit and active when he joined a high school team, and he hadn't forgotten how to run when, in his early twenties, he returned from "retirement." Older beginners can't profit from his experience, he says, but only from his encouragement.

Priscilla Welch has solid advice to offer late starters. She remembers how it felt, having started at "square one" in her midthirties.

In this way, she resembles Jack Foster. He ran only eight years before setting his long-lasting world masters marathon record. "I was getting a little thicker around the waist and made the excuse that there was no 'give' in the modern manmade fibers used in pants," Foster recalls. "One day, I had the bright idea that I'd have a run."

When he returned home a few minutes later, his wife asked, "What's wrong, have you forgotten something?" He wondered what she meant. "You've only been gone about 7 minutes," she said.

"Impossible!" Jack countered. "I'm sure I ran at least 6 or 7 miles." But his wife's watch was correct. The 7 minutes had seemed like 77 to the neophyte runner.

"I began running—only jogging, I now realize—only every second day," he says, "and I was working to maintain that 20-minute jog even on alternate days. But I kept at it."

It's encouraging to know that Jack Foster and Priscilla Welch, both future world record-setters, shared the same early running experiences of most late-starting beginners. Take comfort from these two if you're a master starting to run now.

Training for F-I-Tness

As you set up a first training program, focus on the word "F-I-T." Its letters stand for the three key elements in any training program: *Frequency, Intensity,* and *Time.* Put another way, they answer your three key questions: How often? How hard? and How long?

The following advice applies only to basic training schedules. We'll cover specific tips on preparing to race in chapter 9.

Frequency

Give yourself time off to recover from the new physical demands of training. Renowned track coach Bill Bowerman values rest for all runners. "The well-conditioned runner learns early," he says, "that rest is as important to his or her success as exercise." It becomes even more important as the recovery rate slows with age.

Bowerman's major contribution to training theories was the hard/easy system. Under this system, his competing athletes took a hard workout one day, then eased off the next one to three days before hitting another day hard.

"In 30 years of training national- and world-class runners," Bowerman says, "I found that they progress more rapidly and painlessly with an alternating program of hard and easy. Chronic fatigue states are avoided."

He adapted this method to new runners by recommending a three- or four-day weekly running schedule. Aerobics pioneer Kenneth Cooper, M.D., recommends a similar program: no fewer than three, but no more than five, runs per week.

Intensity

Run slowly, but not too slowly. George Sheehan, M.D., who ranks close to Dr. Cooper in the medical hierarchy of running, says, "If the pace is too slow, it does little good. On the other hand, a too-fast pace is self-defeating."

Dr. Sheehan insists that the body knows, much more precisely than any stopwatch can tell it, what proper pace is. "The most liberating concept in exercise physiology has been the idea of perceived exertion," he says. To explain this concept he refers to a scale that Gunnar Borg, Ph.D., devised to measure the "feel" of exercise.

"Comfortable" and "somewhat hard" are the key words on Dr. Borg's scale, according to Dr. Sheehan. He tells runners to "set your inner dial just below the discomfort zone, then stay there—easing off the pace whenever it starts to hurt and increasing it when it feels too easy."

Find the line between comfort and discomfort, then use it as your pacing guide. If you never nudge that line, you never push it to a higher level. But if you push too far past it, too often, you will break down.

Time

Run long enough, but not too long. If you're running to get most of the physical benefits, "long enough" isn't very long.

For fitness runners, Dr. Cooper puts the upper limit at 3 miles. That takes less than ½ hour to complete and gives maximum aerobic returns with minimum structural problems.

Remember, however, that your mind has somewhat different requirements. The early minutes aren't often pleasant, even for fit athletes who have run for years.

Measuring the Feel of Exertion

According to Dr. Gunnar Borg, you can measure the intensity of your workout by using his Perceived Exertion Scale.

The ratings on Dr. Borg's scale roughly correspond to pulse rates (minus the zeroes) at various levels of exertion for young people. Masters runners normally perceive similar efforts at a lower pulse because their maximum rate declines with age. Choose an effort level for most of your runs that you perceive to be at the "comfortable" to "somewhat hard" level, nudging but not going over the line into discomfort.

Rating	Perception of Effort	Approximate Pulse
7 or less	Very, very light	70 or below
8 and 9	Very light	80–90
10 and 11	Fairly light	100–110
12	Comfortable	120
13 and 14	Somewhat hard	130–140
15 and 16	Hard	150–160
17 and 18	Very hard	170–180
19 and up	Very, very hard	190 and up

This is a time for warming up and for finding the running rhythm. Runners wade through the first mile or two so they can get to the good part, which may not arrive until 30 minutes has passed.

For this reason, plan to run (or run-walk or just walk) for at least 30 minutes — but no more than 60 minutes — right from your first day of training. You do this as much for the head as for the heart, because the longer exercise periods are more satisfying.

Even as you gain fitness and experience, stay in the 30- to 60-minute time frame in most of your training. These runs are long enough to make you want to come back for more but short enough to allow you to do so.

Mixing and Matching Activities

As noted early and often in these pages, age penalizes runners two ways. Masters get hurt more easily and heal more slowly than younger athletes do. Priscilla and Bill are not exempt from these effects of aging.

"For the longest time, I thought I was above injuries," Priscilla says. "Now I know better and have added more supplemental and alternative training to deal with it."

Adds Bill, "I recognize that some other types of aerobic exercise, along with strength training and stretching, are good for avoiding injuries. So I do what I have to do."

Alternative training, supplemental training, cross-training — whatever you wish to call it — fills a greater need the older you get. You need more stretching exercises to fight the tightening of age and more strengthening exercises to correct muscle imbalances. At the same time, you need more time to recover after hard workouts and races, more days off from running, and more optional activities for those days when you don't run. And, if you are injured, you need something to keep yourself active and sane during your recovery.

Yet many runners remain holdouts against cross-training. They think the crossover benefits of bicycling, swimming, weight-training, and the like have been oversold. They side with Mark Covert, a former national-caliber runner from California who has gone more than 20 years without missing a day's run. Covert, who proudly calls himself a "monoathlete," says, "I don't swim, I don't bike, I don't lift weights. I just run."

Bill also notes that "I've never really become a cross-trainer. I haven't used all the different machines or done aerobic dancing. I just don't have the interest, to be honest, in all these new activities. My main interest is still in running, and if I can keep doing that, it's what I prefer. I'm a very traditional runner."

Yet by whatever name he calls his supplemental work, Bill still does some cross-training. He'll discuss exactly what he does later in this chapter.

The Case for Cross-Training

One of the best inventions for runners has been the triathlon. If nothing else, it's given us runners permission to train differently when we can't run.

But while we might appreciate the value of mixing activities, we also recognize the limits of doing so. We long thought we were fooling ourselves if we imagined that anything but more running would improve our running.

Finding Your Fitness Level

Early in your program, you may want to identify your fitness level and how it compares with other people of your age and sex. Dr. Kenneth Cooper, M.D., the man who made the word "aerobics" popular, has conducted extensive tests on beginners for either the distance they can run in 12 minutes or their times for 1½ miles. Dr. Cooper says the results correlate quite closely with those obtained from sophisticated laboratory measurements of basic aerobic fitness.

A mile run (the test that Dr. George Sheehan recommends in chapter 5) gives similar results. The physiological reactions to running 1 mile instead of 1½ miles are quite similar, yet the mile is a much more familiar distance—the most common standard by which runners are measured.

Test yourself by running a mile on a track or carefully measured, flat route. Don't race at full speed, but run—or walk if necessary—at a manageable pace.

Then rate your fitness level by the standards (listed in the table) used in the *Runner's World* National Fun-Run program. Don't take low ratings too seriously. Personal progress is what you seek, and this test merely draws a baseline from which to move to a higher category in tests to follow.

Fitness Level	Sex	Time by Age Group			
		30–39	40–49	50–59	60+
I	Women	8:00	8:30	9:00	9:30
	Men	7:00	7:30	8:00	8:30
II	Women	8:30	9:00	9:30	10:00
	Men	7:30	8:00	8:30	9:00
III	Women	9:30	10:00	10:30	11:00
	Men	8:30	9:00	9:30	10:00
IV	Women	10:30	11:00	11:30	12:00
	Men	9:30	10:00	10:30	11:00
V	Women	10:31+	11:01+	11:31+	12:31+
	Men	9:31+	10:01+	10:31+	11:01+

Swimming makes you a better swimmer, biking a better biker. Likewise, to become a better runner, you must run, and to race fast you must train fast. Training is specific.

Nevertheless, there is one apparent benefit to cross-training. It allows a runner's overtrained legs to recover. Despite this important benefit, it has long been the consensus that true triathletes are the decathletes of endurance sports. Their mixture of training makes them good at everything but great at nothing.

Or so we thought. That conventional wisdom now erodes in the face of new and contrary evidence.

One piece of evidence doesn't directly involve masters but should impress runners of all ages. Faster than you can say "specificity," a prominent triathlete, Erin Baker, made a notable mark in running history.

Baker, a past Ironman Triathlon winner from New Zealand, won the women's category and set a course record at one of America's longest road races, the 1989 Bix Seven in Iowa. It was only her fourth stand-alone race. More impressively, she hadn't forsaken triathlon training to do this. She won a world championship in that sport a week later.

The winner in the Bix Seven was Mark Nenow, who also set a course record. Nenow wasn't a triathlete and didn't intend to become one, but was forced to train on a bike that spring after breaking a foot bone. For six weeks, he substituted hard 50-mile rides for his usual runs.

His transition back into running was easier and faster than he and his doctors expected. After only a few weeks back on his feet, Nenow set personal bests for 3000 meters—twice—and just missed his 5000 PR.

Part of his success came from getting healed, rested, and hungry for competition during his running layoff. But the biking, which builds "speed" muscles in the upper legs and helped him maintain his aerobic capacity, surely contributed to his fastest times in his shortest racing distances. In short, cross-training didn't just keep Nenow from losing his endurance. It also gave him new strength.

Resting By Training

Again we turn to Jack Foster, who, due to his longevity as a runner, has become a fount of knowledge and experience from which others can learn. He brought a bicycle-racing background to running, continued to supplement his training with bike rides (an almost unheard-of practice in the 1970s), and returned to cycling as his primary activity after retiring as a marathoner.

Dr. George Sheehan and Jeff Galloway talk in chapter 6 about their switch to every-other-day running. The only problem this caused them was a vague feeling of guilt at doing nothing as many as four days each week.

Galloway found his relief in water training: not swimming, but "running" in water with support from a flotation belt called the AquaJogger. (The Wet Vest is designed for the same purpose.) Waterwork lets him stay active while giving his legs a needed breather from road-shock. Dick Brown, a physiologist who operates a water-training center in Eugene, Oregon, helped design the AquaJogger and trains athletes as famous as Mary Decker Slaney in the pool.

Slaney suffered another of her frequent injuries one spring, Brown says. "She spent three weeks in the water with no land workouts at all. However, she 'ran' the exact workouts that we had planned for the land in the pool—same length [in time], same effort, same periods of work and recovery for her intervals."

Three days after resuming land training, Slaney set a world 2000-meter record. Brown says that her case isn't unusual. "Runners don't just maintain fitness with water training during the recovery period. Often they actually *gain* fitness. They continue to get excellent cardiovascular workouts while taking away the pounding, and that combination is doubly beneficial."

A colleague of Brown's in Eugene, Stan James, M.D., is one of the country's leading sports physicians. Beyond that, he has trained continuously for one sport or another for 40 years. In his late fifties, he's a talented runner and an even better cross-country ski racer.

"I know what it's like to feel tired all the time," Dr. James says. He always felt that way when he ran every day. He was often sore, too. Now he says, "I think three good-quality workouts a week can maintain a very high fitness level. The training program should have definite peaks and valleys. Not just undulating terrain, so to speak—a little hard and a little easy—but real ups and downs.

"Too many people's 'quality' days aren't all that high quality because they're a little bit tired. Their so-called easy days are a little too hard. They're chronically tired and sore from humming along in the middle someplace."

Dr. James says runners would profit more from "a really good, stimulating, hard effort followed by a *very* minimal effort. My definition of an easy day is not doing something to foul up the quality day, which should be a delightful workout when you feel fresh."

The doctor follows his own prescription. "My health and energy levels have improved since I replaced daily running with every-other-day running. Generally, I feel really good on these runs—light, refreshed."

Dr. James says that he "might be better off staying in bed on the easy days." Yet he, like Jeff Galloway, won't let himself rest completely. As it turns out, he found out that total rest isn't necessary. The only necessity is giving the legs relief from the pounding. We can put in the rest time in other ways besides running—and without that stress on the legs.

"I'll bike, cross-country or roller-ski, swim, or do a weight workout," Dr. James says of his in-between days. "Afterward, I'm a little bit tired but not hurting. If I had run for 2 hours, I'd really be achy, and an injury might even crop up. But I can roller-ski or bike for 2 hours and recover very rapidly. The difference is that I don't pound my legs."

That pounding is the recurring theme here. The inescapable fact of running is that you strike the ground with an average force of three times your body weight. Your body can only absorb so much of that force before it begs for relief.

Relief may take the form of the bicycling that Jack Foster favors, the waterwork preferred by Jeff Galloway, the roller-skiing of Stan James, or even the plain and simple walking that some elite masters runners (including Priscilla Welch) practice.

New Zealander Rod Dixon won an Olympic 1500-meter medal in his twenties and the New York City Marathon in his thirties. At 40, he said, "I used to think the amounts of rest and stress in training should be equal. Now I think the ratio should be three or four times rest to stress."

On some of his stress-avoidance days, Dixon lifts weights, trains in the water with a Wet Vest, mountain bikes, and, yes, even walks.

This last option is the most readily available and often the most overlooked of the low-impact alternatives to running. Training in water, on treadmills, on stationary bikes, or on ski simulators involves degrees of sensory deprivation and takes you nowhere. A bicycle takes you outdoors, but it also puts you in direct competition with auto traffic. But walking is most like running: a slower version of running that takes two or three times longer to cover the same ground, but with a small fraction of the impact.

Dr. James sees the growing acceptance of substitutes among his running patients as a healthy trend. "It's easier to sell runners on this idea of cross-training than it used to be," he says. "There once was a lot of resistance." When Dr. James used to ask them, "Why don't you consider some alternative activity for a while?" they would say, "Are you kidding? No way! I'll either run or do nothing." Now he reports that today the more common response is "Yeah, I've been thinking about that. Maybe I'll swim and bike for a while."

Cross-Training Practices

Priscilla Welch and Bill Rodgers each have tried and continue to try cross-training and can attest to the rewards.

Strength Work

Priscilla says, "I lift weights during winter to balance my hamstrings and quads. I lapsed a little in my weight training between 1987 and 1989, and I knew it when I was beaten in the masters division of the L'eggs 10-K. I just had no strength in my legs that day. We've reviewed my whole training schedule and made it a bit more varied."

And Bill comments, "I've used weights ever since I was in high school. I've always used light weights, not for my legs so much as for my arms, shoulders, and back. I use 12-pound dumbbells, and usually do 30 presses and 30 curls with each arm. I do two sets of those after a running workout.

"I also started doing sit-ups in high school and still do about 50 a day. My other strength exercise, so to speak, is chopping wood.

"That's the way Tarzan Brown, a two-time Boston Marathon champion, used to train for the Boston Marathon. Chopping wood is an old New England training technique."

Running in Water

"I've spent many an hour, during periods of injury, running back and forth in a pool while wearing a Wet Vest," Priscilla explains. "It does become boring, but I think, 'I want to maintain my fitness, so I've got to do this.' I simulate my running workouts in the pool and have spent as long as 2½ hours in there. I come out looking like a prune.

"After training in the pool for several weeks, it takes me another week to get my balance back on land. When I'm not having problems with injuries, I get in the pool only now and again."

Swimming

Bill says, "For recovery after workouts, I sometimes swim around in a pool or pond but don't count laps. I like to go to a pool and leisurely paddle around for 15 minutes.

"When I have injuries, I go in the water and do kicking for my Achilles. I try to get mobility in my ankle area and loosen up my calf muscles."

Treadmill

Priscilla says, "As we're writing, Dave and I just got a treadmill for the house. It's just like the one used by Ingrid Kristiansen, the marathon world record-holder who also lives in Boulder. You can adjust it to simulate hills. We got it for those days when it's too cold and snowy to run well outdoors."

Bicycling

Bill says, "After my long runs nowadays, instead of going for a second run that day, I'll take a short bike ride with my wife and daughter Elise. We do this a lot when we're spending the winter in Phoenix.

"The roads in the Massachusetts town of Sherborn, where I live the rest of the year, are really poor — very potholed and dangerous for a bike. I have an exercise bike that I use a lot, even in summer, as a second workout when I'm hurting from running."

And Priscilla adds, "I do a lot of work on the exercise bike, but like running in the water it can get boring. I'll work on the bike for 15 minutes or so as a warmup when I go to the weight room. I can tolerate it if the television is on or if I can play tapes on a headphone."

Walking

Priscilla states, "I'm a great believer in walking. I grew up walking everywhere, because we didn't have a car and in my little village there was only one bus in and one bus out each day. My little territory was so small that we would walk most places.

"My father was a great walker. He used to work on the farm, walking behind the horse with a plow in his younger days. And after a whole day's work, he would walk from our village to the next, going from one pub to another. He used to cover a lot of ground that way.

"Even today, I walk a lot. I often walk to the shops to get groceries. It's an English sort of thing to do."

9

The Means to the End

What Every Beginner Should Know about Training for Speed and Distance

Priscilla and Bill would be the first to tell you that running for exercise and training to race are two very different activities. The more serious your racing becomes, the less like exercising it is.

The purpose of fitness running is to keep you healthy, and as such it never should feel exhausting or painful. But racing involves pushing your limits, which can feel unpleasant. You can build an immunity to that unpleasantness by gradually adding small doses of it to your training schedule.

The following program leads you into race training. You can adapt it to fit your specific abilities and racing distances.

Keep in mind that a race doesn't really start at the starting line. It begins the day you make the decision to enter a race and make the commitment to train for it. How well you run on race day is the product of what you started doing weeks or even months earlier.

We talked in chapter 8 about the general rules of running. Now we'll talk specifically about race preparation.

Millions of words from experts all over the world have been written on this subject, which can be reduced to the three essential words in any racer's training vocabulary—the three key elements of any sound program:

Long: Adapting to the race distance, which often is farther than you normally run.

Fast: Learning to handle race pace, which usually is faster than you typically go.

Easy: Recovering between the long and fast training sessions and races.

That last word—"easy"—may be the most important, especially for masters, and the least appreciated. More races are lost by training too long, too fast, and too often than by running too little or too easily.

Running Easily

The hardest training for most runners to schedule is the easiest kind. In few other sports is effort so directly linked with accomplishment, so running naturally attracts workaholics. They then are force-fed the most damaging myth in athletics and fitness: "Pain equals gain."

Racing can be—maybe *should be*—uncomfortable, and some training must be directed toward immunizing yourself against that discomfort. You can't improve without it. But no one can stand to train painfully all the time. In that case, all that pain equals is ever-increasing pain—until finally it breaks you down physically or psychologically.

Exciting and challenging as it might be, racing (as well as training that mimics the race in distance or speed) is an unnatural act. It tears you down, and you must build back up after hard efforts by taking easier ones.

Alternately tearing and repairing will eventually make you a better racer, but only if the recovery between hard efforts is adequate. In other words, the easy running makes the hard work *work.*

Elite athletes may alternate hard and easy days. Most masters runners, however, are slower to rebound. One hard session each week, taken as an actual race or as racelike speed or distance work, is about all the older runner can tolerate.

Taking frequent rest days has its merits, as does cross-training with activities such as swimming, bicycling, and walking. Still, recovery doesn't demand complete rest or completely avoiding running altogether. By running easily, you can recover while still satisfying your urge to run. Just remember to stay well within the comfort zone on these days. Most runners train comfortably with runs lasting ½ to 1 hour and with a pace 1 to 2 minutes per mile slower than their race pace for a comparable distance.

These easy runs just aren't the place to increase the length or intensity of your training. As tempting as it may be, save that effort for the long or fast workouts.

The easy runs are the meat and potatoes—or, if you're a vegetarian, the beans and rice—of the running diet. The dessert comes as small, infrequent portions of racing and training at abnormal speeds and distances.

Training Longer

Distance is in the eye of the beholder. One runner's long race may be another's speed test.

Elite athletes who average 15 to 20 miles a day aren't bothered much by even the marathon distance. Running that far fast is their main concern and the major focus of their training.

Experienced racers with less ambition and mileage feel the same way about events lasting less than an hour. They regularly go this far in training, so their aim in racing is to do it faster than usual.

Only when the race distance far exceeds your everyday limits do longer-than-normal training runs become critical. How long? It depends entirely on your goal.

Let's say you're aiming to run a 10-K. That distance becomes your training target. Work up to the race distance by increases no farther than a mile, starting 1 mile above the average distance you currently run. If that is 3 miles, go 4 — but at a pace slower than you normally run.

Before you consider running fast, run long. You'll only need to concern yourself with training for speed if the racing distance is short.

Training Faster

Adding miles to your run is simply a matter of persistence, running farther at the same old pace. Increasing speed, however, is a technical problem that requires a change of your running style.

Five kilometers is a speed test many runners fail, because they suffer from what might be called "one-pace syndrome." They simply never have learned to run fast.

Runners with little background in short-distance racing may never have picked up the techniques—more spring from the ankles, more lift with the knees, longer stride, greater arm action, etc.—so they can't run much faster in races than in training, or in 5-K's than in 10-K's.

Fortunately, even runners who have never learned speedwork can improve their times by adapting their workouts a little at a time. As little as 1 fast mile a week for several weeks can lead to an improvement of 30 seconds or more in a 5-K race.

If you're looking for a speed breakthrough, go to a local track or an accurately measured stretch of flat road once a week for two or more consecutive weekends. Warm up well, then time yourself for a mile. Try to run about 1 minute faster than your everyday pace.

Training for the Fun Run

No author has started more people running than Kenneth Cooper, M.D., author of the aerobics series of books. No authority has researched the subject more thoroughly than Dr. Cooper, whose Aerobics Center in Dallas has collected data on thousands of runners.

Dr. Cooper's work has convinced him that "anyone running more than 15 miles a week is doing it for reasons other than fitness." He sets the upper limit for exercise-runners at 3 comfortably paced miles, five days a week.

Let's say you now stand at Dr. Cooper's upper limit of about five 3-mile runs weekly. Fitness remains important to you, but now you want a little more than exercise. You want to try racing but only in fun runs of about 5-K to 10-K.

The following program takes you one step beyond Dr. Cooper's upper limit. With this step, you make two changes in the program he recommends: Make one run each week longer or faster than before (but not both longer and faster) to prepare for the extra demands of a race. Then, add one more rest day each week to compensate for the extra demands of the harder day.

This program blends the three essential elements of all workable systems:

• Long runs to train you for longer racing distances. Up to twice as far as you normally run, but at a pace slower than normal. (Example for someone who typically runs 3 miles at a 9-minute pace: Go as far as 6 miles and as slow as 10 minutes per mile.)

Say your daily running averages 9 minutes per mile. Try running this mile in about 8 minutes. Go faster than usual, but don't try to make it a race. If you pace it right, you should finish the mile feeling as though you might be able to go several more miles.

The purpose of speed training is to rehearse a full racing pace at only a partial distance. Long training, on the other hand, simulates full distance at a slower pace. Combine the long running with the speed running only when it counts: in the race itself.

Tapering and Recovering

Training has a delayed reaction. You race on the strength and speed developed weeks earlier, not from the last few days before the race. The point

• Fast runs to train you for faster racing paces. Somewhat faster than you normally run, but for less than half your normal distance. (Example for someone who typically runs 3 miles at a 9-minute pace: Warm up with 1 easy mile, run 1 mile as fast as 8 minutes, and then cool down with 1 easy mile.)

• Easy days for recovery between the big weekly efforts. Normal Cooper-style 3-mile runs three days a week, and three rest days weekly. ("Rest" means no running. Cross-training is okay on some days as long as it stays easy.)

The sample weekly schedule below best meets the needs of a fun-runner aiming for a 5-K to 10-K, with at least one long and one fast training run leading up to each race.

Day	Plan
1	Run 3 miles at normal pace.
2	Run 3 miles at normal pace.
3	Rest, or cross-train easily.
4	Run 3 miles at normal pace.
5	Rest, or cross-train easily.
6	Run 4 to 6 miles, slower than normal; *or* run 1 mile, faster than normal, between miles at normal pace; *or* race.
7	Rest, or cross-train easily.

here is that last-minute cramming before a race doesn't help, and in fact may do harm. So limit yourself to easy running the final week before the race. (See more about tapering for races and recovering from them in chapter 12.)

Just as a race doesn't start at the starting line but in the preparation beginning weeks or months earlier, it also doesn't finish at the finish line. It stays with you long after the racing ends. Both the pride and the pain remain.

Later on race day, look at the numbers frozen on the face of your digital stopwatch as you finished, and be proud of them. You alone put them there. Leave the time on the watch until you start your next training run. The act of zeroing it out then signals that the last race is finished and that the next one is beginning. It begins cautiously, with essential repair work. Allow at least one easy day of recovery for each hard mile of racing.

Then commit yourself to a new race and train for it. In this sense, the racing never stops. You're always training for a race, running it, or recovering from it. One event leads directly to the next and then the one after that. This is as it should be. The physical benefits of this sport have a short shelf-life. If you drop off your schedule for more than a few days and lose your momentum, you may begin to detrain—both mentally and physically.

Racing itself has little to do with fitness. But it acts as a motivator to keep people doing the gentler running that does make them fit. In that way, its contribution is enormous.

Pw Priscilla's Experience

I never really felt embarrassed about starting to run at almost 35. I did wonder my first few times out whether I was using the right motions for running, but I soon learned that I didn't look too odd.

I also worried a little bit about making an absolute fool of myself at my first race, where most of the runners were so much younger. But that feeling quickly passed, too, when everyone made me feel welcome.

As I said in chapter 2, I started running with my friend Peggy, the wife of one of my husband's military friends. We would go only a couple of kilometers, and at the end Dave was always waiting to ask, "How did it feel?"

I remember coming back one day and announcing that I could have gone much farther. Dave said, "Okay, that's what I've been waiting to hear." We then made plans for my next step up. We both got down on the floor with a map of the area and talked about how far I would go.

The more I ran, the healthier I felt and the better I raced. But I had started from square one. Track and field and distance running had never appealed to me when I was younger. I was never any good at sports in school and wasn't used to competition. Dave, even after he became my coach, never pushed me. We progressed the sensible way. We didn't start to train seriously and methodically until we heard about the 1981 London Marathon, and then we took all of 1980 to prepare for it. The earlier running had all been something of a lark.

I never imagined then the level that I would reach. We had no designs on that originally. I just enjoyed belonging to a club and looked forward to participating in the club-against-club races, things like that.

My basic advice to women who are beginning late is to do exactly as I did: Just start with a short distance, and don't run hard. You need only to tootle around in training. After you get a lot of aerobic running under your belt, then start playing around with the speed.

If you haven't run before, start off slowly, gently, and easily. Run as far as is comfortable, then walk a bit—jog, walk, jog, walk. For instance, go to a local high school track and jog one lap in the far outside lane, then move in one lane and walk the next lap, and so on.

Set yourself little goals: 1 mile or 2 miles, and walk if you have to. There's no disgrace in that. Even Ingrid Kristiansen, the world marathon record-holder, occasionally walks up hills in her workouts. ■

BR Bill's Encouragement

Maybe I'm not the best person to be giving advice to older beginners, since I've never been one. I started running in my teens when I already was in pretty good shape, and slipped away from running only for a little while in my early twenties.

The best thing I can offer might be encouragement. Anyone starting to run should begin by congratulating himself or herself. Too many people downplay what they've done by saying, "I only ran this," or, "I only raced that." I always tell them that it's great they're out there doing something.

You've got to be positive. What you've done by taking steps to be fit is worth more than a million dollars in the bank. It makes such huge changes in your life.

You've got to build up your running gradually, over weeks and even months. Otherwise, you get sore and tired and discouraged. Someone could run for the first 38 days straight and think that's a great start. But it makes more sense to run only a few times a week in the beginning.

Beginners should train by a pattern that competitive runners use: a hard/easy system. We don't train hard every day, but take easy runs between the big efforts. Since every run is pretty hard at first, beginners should take at least one day off between runs. If you want to work out aerobically on those days off, you can bike, swim, or walk. These activities are easier on the body but still give good results.

Specific exercise programs are individual matters, but there are certain parameters. Every runner, regardless of how experienced, requires one to three days to recover from a hard workout. The beginner especially should know this rule and observe it.

I tell people at running clinics that a training program is worth the most when you can do just a little bit consistently. Take a low-key, long-term approach rather than an "I have to do everything now" approach. ■

10

Racing for Fun

How to Start, How to Finish

You can be a novice racer at any age. Bill Rodgers ran his first race at 15, but Priscilla Welch didn't enter hers until she was almost 35. You can be a master by the calendar yet still be a neophyte at racing. It's never too late to be a beginner.

If you're tempted to race, this chapter will lead you gently into the organized sport. We assume that you've already taken a runner's longest step: that is, into running. The second-longest is the one you're now thinking of taking: to the starting line of a race.

Reasons to Race

The thought of racing both intrigues and intimidates you. You've been running for a while and have graduated from the first trudges around the block to comfortable half-hour runs. You're looking for a new challenge. You watched the big local race last year and thought, "Maybe I could . . ."

Then the dream gives way to doubts: "What if I finish last? What if I can't finish at all? What if I look silly in front of my family, friends, and neighbors?"

Should you race? Only if you're convinced that you'll be a more complete runner with racing than without it. If you enjoy running for the solitude it offers, and if you feel no urge to increase distances and improve times, racing offers you little. But if you yearn to mix with other runners both as companions and competitors, and if you're eager to test your mileage and speed limits, you're ready to go public with your running.

Try one race—just for fun. Otherwise, you'll never know whether racing attracts or repels you. Like many runners, you may find that the companionship and competition can spur you on to better your personal bests. More often than not, runners get caught up in the excitement of these events and come back for more.

Choosing a Race That's Right for You

Find a race that won't discourage you, at a distance you're capable of finishing. Races come in many shapes and sizes: road, track, and cross-country races; big and small ones; short and long ones; and hilly and flat ones.

As a new racer, you'll probably fit most comfortably into a 5-kilometer road race. It's the shortest distance commonly run, and it's the perfect length for beginners. Later, you can advance to 8-K's, 10-K's, and beyond if you like.

Translating from Metric to Miles

Most races are measured under the metric system, so American runners must learn to convert these distances from miles.

One kilometer (commonly abbreviated "K") equals 1000 meters or 62 percent of a mile.

The mile is the only distance from the U.S. standard of measurement in which world and national records can still be set. It's equal to 1609 meters. (Some road races, however, also go 5 miles—8.05 kilometers—and 10 miles—16.1 kilometers). A marathon, an odd distance in either system, is 26.22 miles or 42.19 kilometers. The half-marathon obviously is exactly half as far.

Here are the standard events and their mile equivalents.

Event	Equivalent (mi.)
1500	0.93
3-K	1.86
5-K	3.11
8-K	4.97
10-K	6.21
12-K	7.46
15-K	9.32
20-K	12.43
25-K	15.54
30-K	18.64
50-K	31.08

Choose a popular road race, because these events draw the most runners, many of them first-timers like yourself. You want the largest and most varied supporting cast possible for your first race. That way, you can both hide in the crowd and catch its contagious excitement.

Avoid track and cross-country races for now, since these are small and serious. Running with competitors who are far more experienced might sour you on racing at the start.

Today's mass-participation road races can be fun if you approach them in the spirit that dominates these events. You "win" on your own terms. To you, that may mean completing the course, running farther than you ever have before, or holding a faster pace.

Preparing to Race

If you've never raced before, you'll find that winning is easy — because finishing *is* winning. Still, if you are like most beginners and have a fear of finishing last, remember that no matter how slow you are, there'll always be someone slower — someone who didn't do their homework like you did.

Prepare yourself for the distance of the race and for its pace. Both may take you beyond the normal limits of your usual training runs, so you'll have to adapt your schedule a bit. If you plan to race a 10-K, for instance, take at least one practice run of 6 miles or more but at an easier pace than you intend to race. You will also need to experience the feel of a full race pace at least once in training, but be sure to run at that pace for only a *portion* of the racing distance. The only time you should combine the two elements — full pace for the full distance — is in the race itself.

Also, limit the number of new experiences on race day. Wear the shoes and clothes that you know are comfortable from having trained in them, and eat (or don't eat) as you normally would before any run.

Go to the race (and perhaps run it) with an experienced advisor. This sport is all new to you, so it may be a little frightening. Someone who has been there at least once before can steady you.

The Right Racing Moves

Survival is the best first measure of success for a novice in this game. Surviving the distance comes from equal parts of preparation and restraint. Even if you've done everything right in training, you can undo all that good with as little as one wrong move on race day.

The most common rookie mistake is leaving the starting line too quickly. Start in midpack or farther back. Serious race veterans zoom away from the starting line very quickly, trampling anyone who gets in their way.

Start slowly. Resist getting caught up in the opening rush. Later in the race, when it's much more fun to pass than to be passed, you'll see many of those overeager novices who dashed off early. As you breeze by them, you'll discover a sense of satisfaction for sticking to your strategy rather than having yielded to the exhilaration of the start.

Run to finish. That's your first goal. Keep the pace conservative to assure yourself a good first experience.

The Point of the PR

Once you've dampened your feet in racing by sampling an organized event, why not jump in all the way? See how much faster you can run this distance than you did the first time.

After just one race, you now have a PR, a "personal record," a standard on which to base your improvements. Your PR is an individual yet objective way to measure your success and progress. Improving it doesn't depend upon beating anyone but yourself.

Be proud of your PR, but not so proud that you want to preserve it. Your record, like all records, is made to be broken. No one can break it for you, and no one can take it from you.

The PR is the only race prize that really means anything. T-shirts and certificates are awarded to anyone who pays an entry fee, and the nationally recognized elite can get paid just for showing up. Records, on the other hand, must be earned.

You win them the way all athletes do: by preparing better than your "opponent"—in this case, your current PR—and then racing smarter. (We'll discuss how to refine your training and pacing in chapter 11.)

Meanwhile, here are a few tricks to shave seconds off your time.

Pick your spots. Race most seriously in the spring or fall, when the weather is likely to be most favorable for a fast time (a temperature in the 50s is ideal). Choose a flat course designated "certified," one that has passed stringent measurement tests and is certain not to yield inaccurate times.

Warm up. Think how sluggish you feel in the first couple of miles of your daily runs. You don't want to labor through most of your 5-K that way, so work those kinks out before the race starts by jogging *easily* for 10 to 20 minutes.

Time yourself. Start your watch as *you* cross the starting line, not when the gun sounds. The seconds or even minutes spent shuffling up to the line become part of your time in the results kept by race officials, but you shouldn't count it against you.

Cut corners. Don't run as if you were driving, always staying in the right-hand lane and making proper turns. Race courses are measured along the shortest possible route that a runner could travel, so you can actually penalize yourself by straying from that path.

Compete. Realize that your finishing position ultimately means little, but still use the people in front of you as moving targets. After the starting rush is over and runners have settled into their paces, reel them in one after another. Once you've landed the one in front of you, set your sights on the next one. This tactic keeps your momentum going and ultimately helps you race faster.

PW Priscilla on Beginning Racing

As I mentioned in chapter 2, the most difficult part about running my first race was getting up my confidence to enter. My husband, Dave, had to twist my arm to get me going, because I thought I would be whitewashed by the younger girls who were fit from their cross-country skiing.

It wasn't long before I entered my first marathon. Many people do one marathon, then never run another because it hurts so much the first time. Yet they talk about the experience the rest of their lives.

This might have happened to me because I went into my first marathon so ill-prepared. Here's how I ended up in one so soon after beginning running. At an all-comers track meet in Oslo (at the legendary Bislett stadium that I didn't yet know was famous), I was running the 3000 meters. I was plodding along next to last, just putting one foot in front of the other. Johan Kagestad, Ingrid Kristiansen's coach, was watching the race with Dave. Johan asked, "Have you ever tried her in a marathon? With the economical way she runs for a first-year runner, she would probably be a good marathoner."

Later, we were going on holiday to Stockholm, where Dave was going to run a marathon. When he registered for it, so did I.

When we registered, the press interviewed us. We saw the story but couldn't read Swedish. Friends who knew the language burst out laughing when they read the headline, "Love Brought Them to Stockholm." The press portrayed us as just a nice little couple running together.

After running the marathon, we both were so stiff and sore that we had to walk down steps sideways. It could have been the perfect excuse to avoid ever attempting anything so foolhardy again, but instead I set my goals on running a faster marathon—*much* faster.

My time at Stockholm was 3:26. Back in our room after the race I said, "Wouldn't it be nice if I could take 1 hour off that time?" It was actually a very naive comment. It wasn't "I'm going to do it," but "Wouldn't it be nice?" I actually had no idea how good a 2:26 marathon was, although at the time it was about 6 minutes faster than the world record. So improving by an hour became my objective. And I did it.

I certainly don't recommend starting off with a marathon as your first race. This distance should come much further along in your evolutionary process as a runner than it did for me.

Go for the short races at first, and then gradually build up. Now there are 5-K's everywhere, and I recommend them for people who are new to racing. A 3-K might be even better. Many of the longer races now also offer a short fun-run of 1 to 3 miles, which is a great place to start.

A fun-run should be exactly that. It's only when you're racing that special types of training and tactics are important.

Experiment in the first race. Get a feel for the atmosphere of racing without taking it too seriously. The serious racing can come later. And even if it never comes, you can keep having fun at these events. ∎

BR Bill on Beginning Racing

I began my running career in a very low-key way. My first race was 1 mile at a Parks and Recreation track meet when I was 15.

When I joined my high school cross-country team, I ran maybe 1½ to 2 miles a day. The team provided me with the type of social structure that would help any beginner.

It's hard to take up running and keep it up all by yourself. You can run alone, but it's easier and more fun if you can draw support from and share experiences with other runners.

Young runners often can find this kind of group support with a high school or college team. Masters runners may find it through running clubs, but the most common source is the races. Our sport now offers a lot of social opportunities. Jeff Galloway, a friend from my college days and a former Olympian, now conducts one of the many camps for runners. Thom Gilligan of Boston promotes international group travel through his company, Marathon Tours.

Gilligan met his future wife through running, and that's also how I met mine. Gail and I met in New York City, where she was running with the Central Park Track Club.

You can't necessarily look forward to finding a spouse this way! But if you join a club or start running races, you immediately make friends with the same interests. To me, these friendships are what running is all about.

As Priscilla says, the beginning racer should look for an event that isn't very long or overly competitive. The best way to get into racing is to choose low-key road races, where the maximum distance is 5-K.

Stick with this limit for the first few months, then experiment with the 10-K. After that, you might want to experiment with the more sophisticated and demanding training methods that we'll discuss in later chapters.

In your first race, fight the tendency to start too fast. It's good to be cautious and say, "My goal is just to finish." And you don't have to think about running a specific time in your first race. Whatever time you run here will be a personal record, and you can concentrate on breaking it on the next try.

A great way to ease into racing is at an event like the Jingle Bell Run that I help conduct in Boston every December. It grew out of something my team-mates and I used to do in high school. We ran at night to see all the Christmas lights. In the late 1970s, 10 or 15 runners got together one year for a run to look at the lights on Boston Common. They were beautiful, and we all sang Christmas carols as we ran. That tradition continued as the Jingle Bell Run. It grew by word of mouth to its current limit of 3,000 runners (who contribute as part of this event between $35,000 and $50,000 a year to Special Olympics). It's totally noncompetitive.

My hope is that Jingle Bell Runs will spring up in every city. It's events like this that excite people about running.

Running shouldn't be all serious, hard work. We need some fun and celebration in our sport. ■

11

Breaking Personal Records

Learn the Steps to Stepping Up Your Pace

Bill and Priscilla are professional athletes. They train to compete and win, not to stay fit.

"Fitness is a stage you pass through on the way to becoming an athlete," says *Runner's World* columnist George Sheehan, M.D. Of course, good health and fitness are the foundation for all racing programs. But eventually for every runner, fitness becomes more a by-product of your running and less a prime motive.

By now, you've entered your first races just to participate. Now you're hooked. You want to race faster, longer, and more often, but you want to keep your running in a healthy context. You want to improve as a racer but without making it seem like a second job. To strike such a balance, you still train much like an exercise-runner on weekdays but like an athlete on the weekends. On that one hard day a week, the key word becomes "more": more distance training, more speed training, and more racing.

As you progress, your racing moves from 12-K, to 15-K, to 10 miles, to the half-marathon. Accordingly, your long training runs grow even longer as you prepare for the extended racing distances.

You need little special instruction to run longer (at least not until you train extra-long for a marathon; see training plans for that event in chapters 12 and 16). You're just doing more of what you already did. Distances grow nicely as long as you remember to increase them gradually and hold down the pace.

Increasing your speed, however, is a more technical exercise. In this chapter, we'll discuss two methods that will improve your time without drastically altering your training program.

Race Improvement Program

This suggested program grows out of several assumptions: (1) You have already taken the first step into racing, using a program such as the one outlined in chapter 10; (2) you now want to improve at racing, both increasing your distances and lowering your times, but also want to remain healthy in the process; (3) you can't or won't allot more than one day a week to extra-long or extra-fast training; (4) your racing range now extends from 5-K (3.1 miles) to half-marathon (13.1 miles); and (5) you are a masters runner and therefore must pay extra attention to recovery time between harder efforts.

The improvement program contains these elements:

1. Long runs up to the distance of your longest race. Run up to a minute per mile slower than normal race pace for this distance.

2. Fast runs—your choice between 1 mile at about 5-K race pace and a 20-minute tempo run (see "Upping the Tempo" on the opposite page) at slightly slower than 10-K race pace. (In both workouts, warm up and cool down well with easier running.)

3. Easy runs of 5-K to 10-K at about 1 minute per mile slower than 10-K race pace.

By alternating long runs with fast runs, you're prepared to race at any distance from 5-K to half-marathon. Recover between once-a-week hard efforts with a minimum of three easy runs and three optional-activity days. The options are (1) an easy run of about 5-K; (2) cross-training with bicycling, swimming, and the like, or (3) rest.

A sample weekly schedule follows.

Day	Plan
1	Optional day: easy 5-K run, cross-training, or rest
2	Easy run: 5-K to 10-K, much slower than race pace
3	Easy run: 5-K to 10-K, much slower than race pace
4	Optional day: easy 5-K run, cross-training, or rest
5	Easy run: 5-K to 10-K, much slower than race pace
6	Big day: race—5-K to half-marathon, *or* long run—half-marathon at slower than race pace, *or* fast run—1 mile at about 5-K race pace, *or* tempo run—20 minutes at about 10-K race pace
7	Optional day: easy 5-K run, cross-training, or rest

Winning by a Mile

All it takes is 1 mile of your weekly schedule to better your time. If your time has reached a plateau, a mile speed run may be just what you need to break the barrier. Shortly before turning 40, Marlene Cimons faced a dilemma common to runners who begin racing late. She began slowly—and had stayed slow.

Cimons, a nationally known writer whose byline appears regularly in running magazines and in the *Los Angeles Times,* was a one-pace runner. She ran about the same pace in races as in training and in 10-K's as in marathons.

"I can run forever," she said then. "But my times in the 10-K have stalled." She was stuck at 52 minutes—a pace of about 8½ minutes a mile.

She'd never trained fast. But in desperation she made one simple change in her routine. Once a week, she ran just 1 mile (after a couple of miles' warmup) 1 minute or so faster than her normal pace. Her first attempts at a 7:30 pace or faster left her breathless and sore, but she persisted with the new routine for a month.

Cimons then entered another 10-K race and bettered her PR by almost 3 minutes—an improvement of about 30 seconds per mile! No one can promise you improvements as dramatic, but this simplest of speed workouts can give you the final push that lifts you out of a pace rut.

Upping the Tempo

Ken and Lisa Martin were once the number one couple of marathoning. They've now divorced, but they still share the same coach and advisor.

Lisa and Ken started working with Jack Daniels, Ph.D., when he served as exercise physiologist for the Athletics West track club in Eugene, Oregon. Now he works with them from his current base at State University of New York in Cortland.

With Dr. Daniels' guidance, Lisa won the 1988 Olympic silver medal in the marathon for Australia. She also collected two Commonwealth Games titles. Ken placed second in the 1989 New York City Marathon with the fastest time (2:09:38) any American had run in six years.

One key peg on which Dr. Daniels hangs his system is aerobic-threshold training. It often goes by the nickname "tempo running."

He defines the aerobic threshold as "the pace beyond which your blood begins to accumulate lactic acid at an accelerated rate. Find a way to raise your lactic acid threshold, and you can run longer at a faster speed."

How do you do this? By finding your training tempo. Dr. Daniels bases the tempo on your most recent 10-K race time plus 20 seconds per mile. For example, if you raced at 7 minutes per mile, you would tempo train for 20 minutes at a 7:20 pace. Tempo running avoids the tendency to train as far as you can, as fast as you can. It helps you train at an even pace so you'll run more evenly in a race.

"Don't turn your threshold-pace workouts into competitive efforts," Dr. Daniels says. "Instead, try to become aware of the fact that you're running the same pace with less effort."

He adds that these runs "should feel comfortably hard" and "should last about 20 minutes. Going too fast on a tempo run is no better than going too slow,

---

Speed Runs

One of the simplest ways to increase your speed is to run a single mile at 5-K race pace once a week. Below is a list of paces for various race times. Find your 5-K PR on the list, then run your speed mile at the corresponding pace. Remember to precede the mile with an adequate warmup run and to cool down properly afterward.

5-K	Mile Pace
15:00	4:50
15:30	5:00
16:00	5:10
16:30	5:19
17:00	5:29
17:30	5:39
18:00	5:49
18:30	5:58
19:00	6:08
19:30	6:17
20:00	6:27
20:30	6:37
21:00	6:46
21:30	6:56
22:00	7:06
22:30	7:16
23:00	7:25
23:30	7:35
24:00	7:44
24:30	7:54

Tempo Runs

Dr. Jack Daniels calls the tempo run one of the most valuable workouts for racers. It's a simple routine he developed to improve your pace and make a remarkable change in your race times.

Use the table to find the time closest to your most recent 10-K race. Run at the corresponding tempo on a track (400 meters or ¼ mile). It should take 20 minutes. Warm up and cool down thoroughly with slower running before and after the tempo work.

10-K Race	Tempo per Mile	Distance in 20 Minutes (laps)
31:00	5:20	15
32:00	5:30	14
33:00	5:40	14
34:00	5:50	13
35:00	6:00	13
36:00	6:10	12
37:00	6:20	12
38:00	6:30	12
39:00	6:40	11
40:00	6:45	11
41:00	6:55	11
42:00	7:05	11
43:00	7:15	11
44:00	7:25	10
45:00	7:35	10
46:00	7:45	10
47:00	7:55	10
48:00	8:05	9
49:00	8:15	9
50:00	8:25	9

and neither is as beneficial as running the proper pace. You could perform a longer-than-20-minute tempo run, but 20 minutes has been shown to produce positive results and will leave you relatively fresh for the next day's training.

"Threshold-pace training," Dr. Daniels advises, "has worked for all my runners, and I'm certain it can work for you. If you give it a try for several weeks, I think you'll find more spring in your stride and an increased enthusiasm in your training."

Bill on Improving

A few years ago, I met a man at a marathon who told me that he was trying the 26.2-mile distance for the first time that day. I asked what his longest run had been.

"Twelve miles," he told me. He was soon to learn that his training was woefully inadequate.

You learn a lot from your first race at any distance. I started racing so long ago that I can barely remember what those early high school events taught me. But the memories of my first marathon are still clear.

It was the 1973 Boston Marathon. The lesson I learned that day was that I'd set too many goals and set them too high.

I now know that it's better to err on the side of caution in your first marathon. But in my first marathon, I aimed for both a high place and a fast time.

The Boston Marathon appealed to me as a starting place because I had seen other people run it earlier. At the time, I was starting to run again and was still trying to quit smoking.

The marathon had always seemed monumental to me. It should appear that way to anyone who runs it, that is, it should scare you into realizing that you can't go into it unprepared.

I thought I'd prepared well enough. Running 100 miles a week by 1973, I had placed well in 20-K and 30-K races leading up to the Boston Marathon in April.

In all my races, going back as far as high school, I had always run to win. So at Boston, I took off with the intention of winning. I aimed to run 2:20 and started too fast.

It was a warm day, and at the time, there wasn't water available at every mile as people now have come to expect in marathons. I became dehydrated. Suddenly, I wasn't feeling well, and I quit.

The marathon had been such a miserable experience that I stopped running completely for two months afterward. I even drove to California, thinking that I would move there and train.

All I needed instead was to learn more about the marathon distance. In fact, I still had a lot to learn about running in general.

When I arrived back in New England, I started to train again. I decided I needed to build up my strength and improve in shorter races before trying the marathon again.

After my disastrous first marathon, I ended up winning my second one— the now-defunct Bay State race at Framingham, Massachusetts—in the fall of 1973. I stayed relaxed for the first 16 miles, just running and talking with a friend, and really only picked up a racing pace for the last 10 miles. With a couple of miles to go, I caught the leaders and went on to win in 2:28:12.

I was happy with my time but more pleased just to have finished. By relaxing and not having too many expectations, I learned that I could enjoy the experience.

I mainly wanted to have one positive experience in a marathon before running Boston again. Returning to the scene of my dropout the year before, I placed 14th with 2:19:34 in 1974. Then in 1975, I won the Boston Marathon in an American-record time of 2:09:55.

This improvement didn't come all on its own. I'd joined the Greater Boston Track Club in 1974 and was coached by Bill Squires. By training under his guidance and with other runners, I learned to push myself properly.

Now I'm with the Brooks Racing Team, which is different from a traditional club in that the members live all over the country and usually only see each other at races. I still have training partners from the old days with the Greater Boston Track Club.

If you haven't already joined a club, do so. You learn a great deal about improving your training and racing by exchanging information with other club members.

I also learn a lot from reading and still read everything I can about running. I like to read different points of view, from the hard-core preachings of Australian coach Percy Cerutty to the low-key approach of author Jeff Galloway.

Running has far more to offer than a daily 3-mile tour of the neighborhood. You can reach high levels of performance by doing the right mix of training: longer and faster work to build you up, plus enough rest and recovery in between to keep you from breaking down. ■

Pw Priscilla on Improving

One sure way to improve quickly is by finding a good coach to guide your training and racing. I was lucky in this regard. Dave helped me from the start, later became my husband, and remains my coach to this day.

Every runner can use a coach or advisor. No matter how experienced you might be, you're often blind to the flaws in your program. You need someone more objective than you are to turn to for counseling.

Of course, finding a coach is easier said than done. Nearly all of the professional coaches in the United States are connected with high school and college teams, and they don't often have the time to work with masters runners.

Many people think they know enough about distance running to coach other runners, but few of them actually know how. More and more of these people are calling themselves coaches, and it's almost tragic.

When we were visiting Gainesville, Florida, two men came to Dave and said they wanted to become coaches. They wanted Dave to tell them everything he knew about coaching. They thought they could pick up in a 1-hour interview what Dave has taken more than 20 years to learn.

Dave is happy to share information with anyone who asks for it. But he warns that a brief talk only scratches the surface of the subject.

At one of our clinics in Toronto, he spoke for well over an hour. In that time, he just covered the basics. He would have loved to have told the crowd everything he knew, but that would have been impossible. I've lived with him and run for him for 15 years, and I still don't know as much as he does about running.

At clinics, we try to give basic formulas in as short a time as possible. It's almost a cookbook recipe approach that gives people an idea of how our system works.

We tell them about two different kinds of programs. Dave calls them "complex training" and "periodization training."

Complex training is the kind used by runners who want to race year-round at a variety of distances. It's the all-purpose training that this chapter emphasizes.

Periodization training is the kind used by runners who want to peak for a particular racing distance or season of the year. Chapter 12 deals with this more focused way of training.

Basically, in complex training you want to develop your aerobic system through longer, slower runs, and you want to increase your anaerobic threshold through shorter, faster runs. You key the length and pace of these runs to the distance and speed of your racing.

The most common distance that a year-round road racer runs is the 10-K. Although this is an aerobic event, it leans more toward anaerobic than the longer races do, so you've got to do more fast work to prepare for it. You don't want to become so hung up on running easy miles that you ignore the need for speed.

You need tempo runs of the type that Dr. Jack Daniels recommends and shorter runs such as a 1-mile at faster than 10-K race pace. You may need 1000-meter or 800-meter intervals (which we introduce in chapter 12). If you've done no fast training and you start spending as little as one day a week on the track, you'll probably experience dramatic improvements in just a few weeks.

But it's also possible to do too much speedwork—and especially too much racing. With as many as eight races a weekend to choose from in metropolitan areas, many runners overrace. They also may end up "racing" in their training.

This again is where a coach can step in. Good coaches can show runners what they sometimes can't see for themselves: when they need more work, when they need less, and when they need a different type. ■

12

Running Faster, Farther, Better

Focusing Your Training for the Best Performance Ever

Priscilla Welch and Bill Rodgers both have made Olympic teams. Both have set world and national records. Both have raced just the way they'd planned on just the right day.

This is called "peaking." It's aiming at one specific goal and then working up to it in a systematic way.

Let's say that up until now you haven't peaked. You've raced a little of this and a little of that across a wide range of distances.

You've entered whatever race came along, whenever it came in the year. You've trained on a regular schedule, but not on one geared toward producing a peak effort.

We now point you toward such an effort, one race or a series of races within one season of the year. To reach your peak, you focus your training on one distance or a tight range of distances. Your work becomes more specific, concentrated, and purposeful.

Going for Distance

Aiming just to finish a marathon doesn't appear, at first glance, to fit the theme of peaking. But think about it: You can't wake up on race day and decide to run this distance the way you can a 10-K. You must build up to a marathon for several months—*peak* for it, in other words.

New marathoners have profited in recent years from the collective wisdom of Jeff Galloway and Tom Osler, two of the sport's most authoritative authors.

Galloway, a former Olympian, tells them to take fewer but longer runs, and Osler, a national champion long-distance runner, tells them to take walks.

Galloway's widely used program has two cornerstones: a very long run once every two to three weeks, increasing by gentle steps—1 mile or less per week—from just above one's current peak on up to the marathon distance, and about half as long on intervening weekends. The second is lots of "filler" between the big efforts, resting one or more days a week and running easily on the other days "to make sure you recover between long ones."

Galloway says he recommends this program because it avoids much of the risk of typical marathon training (which emphasizes more running on more days per week) while still giving excellent results. "Hundreds of 3-mile-a-day runners have shown me they can finish the marathon without 'hitting any wall,'" he says.

Increasing maximum distance safely would normally take a long time on Galloway's formula of advancing by 1 mile or less per week. However, you can alter that formula and still stay healthy.

Tom Osler tells how. He believes that anyone, without any special preparation, can instantly double his or her longest nonstop distance. If you run a steady 10-K, for example, you can reach 20-K *today.*

The trick, says Osler, is to take walking breaks. "No way," you might think. "I've had to walk in my runs, and I can hardly start again." That's because exhaustion forced you to stop.

Osler's breaks are different. You take them voluntarily, *before* you tire, as a means of stretching available resources. You run 15, 20, or 25 minutes, then walk 5. You accomplish larger amounts of work by breaking it into small pieces than by tackling it all at once. (See "Distance Plans" on the opposite page for a routine that combines Osler's and Galloway's methods.)

Begin writing your own program by estimating the time it will take to finish your marathon. You can figure the time by using your most recent 10-K result. A marathon is 4.2 times longer than a 10-K, but most runners take 4.65 times longer to finish. To estimate your first marathon time, therefore, multiply your 10-K time by 4.65. Let's say you ran a 0:45:00 10-K. If you multiply 45 minutes by 4.65, you get 209.25 minutes—or about 3½ hours.

That 3½ hours then becomes your training goal, to be met before race day.

Don't worry about how much distance you cover in that time period. It will surely be less than the full 26.2 miles. That doesn't matter. What counts is getting used to the idea and feel of spending 3½ hours on your feet.

Say you hope to run 3½ hours in the marathon, and your longest training run now is 1 hour. How do you move from your current level to your new goal?

Distance Plans

A runner's first peak experience in long distances probably will be the marathon. Your goal as a first-time marathoner should be to finish without hitting the wall.

With that aim in mind, put aside thoughts of speed for now—both in the marathon and in the training for it. Concentrate on mimicking the experiences of the marathon in your weekly distance runs.

Estimate your marathon finish time (be conservative), then work up to that time on your long runs. Consider taking 5-minute walking breaks every half hour during these sessions to increase your distances quickly and to decrease recovery periods afterward.

Run extra-long once every two to three weeks. In between, add one semilong run at your predicted marathon pace for half the time of the previous extra-long session.

Spend the time between extra-long and semilong runs recovering. Take only easy runs of 30 to 60 minutes and frequent rest days.

The following sample program lasts three months. It best suits runners who start at long runs of about an hour and expect a marathon time of 3½ to 4 hours. Adjust the program's length and its recommended amounts of running if your needs fall outside these ranges.

Note the week's break in midprogram as the long runs grow tougher and the three-week taper between the longest training run and the marathon.

Chapter 16 contains a program for improving marathon times.

Week	Big Day
1	1½ to 2 hours with walks
2	Half of last run without walks
3	2 to 2½ hours with walks
4	Half of last long run without walks
5	2½ to 3 hours with walks
6	Half of last long run without walks
7	3 to 3½ hours with walks
8	Nothing long
9	Half of last long run without walks
10	3½ to 4 hours with walks
11	Nothing long
12	Nothing long
13	Marathon race

Build toward that target amount by ½-hour steps, starting with 1½ hours. Two weeks from now, step up to 2 hours, and so on.

If the amounts and the progress rates sound imposing, adopt Tom Osler's walking breaks. If you don't like the word "walk," think of it as another application of interval training. Intervals break a large chunk of work into smaller pieces to make them more manageable.

Besides increasing your distance this way, you also maintain a faster pace during the running portions than you can without breaks, and you recover more quickly than you could without taking the walks.

The walks are a training technique. Aim to eliminate them on race day, when the excitement of the event will probably energize you enough to make walking unnecessary. But if you still need the breaks during the marathon, take them. If your only goal is to cover the distance, use any trick that will take you to the finish line.

Going for Speed

George Young, at age 34 the oldest American to break the 4-minute mile, knows all about speedwork. He was also the first American distance runner to compete in four Olympics—from 1960 to 1972, the last at age 35. He's now a successful coach at Central Arizona College.

"There's no better way to do speedwork than to run a race," says Young. "You talk of speedwork in terms of interval quarter-miles and all those other things. But you don't get the speedwork there that you gain in a race. You just never really reach the pain barrier, or whatever you call it, in any other way than running the race and hurting that way."

Essentially, Young's method is racing-as-training. Doing the real thing is the best way to improve at it. Still, there are other training methods that are also successful. The key is that they all focus on one concept: The more closely the training resembles the race, the more beneficial it will be. In training terms, this means a runner needs to practice at close to race distance, race speed, or both. Your training should be focused and specific.

Take Norm Green, a Baptist minister, for example. Few runners, masters age or younger, get more from their training miles than he. Green started running in his late forties, and by age 52 he ran a 2:25:51 marathon, the current American record for runners over 50. He still continues to run near 2:30 in his late fifties.

Yet, Green averages less than 60 miles a week, and he rarely trains more than 10 miles at a time. But his routine works, because he does all his training at or near race pace (sub-6:00 miles) and takes his longest runs only in races.

Of course, more-from-less does not mean something-for-nothing. Green clearly is a hard worker, as well as an efficient one who makes every mile count. He finds this race pace method works well for him. It's similar to Jack Daniels' tempo running. (See "Upping the Tempo" on page 93.)

To help a runner break into a faster pace using the tempo method, Dr. Daniels varies the tempo theme by adding what he calls "cruise intervals" to the peaking runner's bag of tricks. Interval training breaks up a block of distance into smaller pieces by inserting recovery periods of jogging and walking. Cruising implies running the fast segments at a tolerable pace, not top speed.

"Plenty of scientific evidence, not to mention common sense, tells you that you can run longer at a certain pace if you take short rests than you can by running that pace nonstop," Dr. Daniels says. "This type of intermittent run/rest approach also reduces the stress level of training."

Dr. Daniels advises running these interval sessions at or near 10-K race pace, certainly no faster. You will still benefit if you run as much as 20 seconds per mile slower. "I generally recommend the 1-mile distance for cruise intervals but believe that any distance from ½ to 2 miles would prove equally effective," he says.

"How many cruise intervals can you do on each hard day? The general rule of thumb is that they should total no more than 8 percent of your total weekly mileage. If, for example, you run 20 miles a week, run about 1½ miles of cruise intervals. If you run 50 miles, do about 4 miles."

Dr. Daniels adds that "a short walk or jog between intervals is essential to the workout, but it should last only 30 to 60 seconds."

You can vary the distance of intervals, their number and pace, and the length of the rest period. The key to making intervals work is to run at the pace you would use in your next race. (See "Speed Plans" on page 104.)

Scheduling Your Peaks

Working harder is one way to get more distance and speed from yourself. Working *smarter* is another way, and you can often do that by simply rearranging your schedule: Adopt seasons of racing, taper the work load before racing, and recover fully after racing.

Find Your Season

You can't race at your best year-round. Racing energies ebb and flow with the seasons.

Tom Osler, author of *The Serious Runner's Handbook,* maintains that runners race best and stay healthiest if they emphasize racing and hard training in certain seasons and avoid these stresses in others. Osler says that highs tend to come in the spring and fall, and the lows in winter and summer.

With so many races now being scheduled in so many places, you could race

---

Speed Plans

If you race often enough and at the right distances, you may not need any extra training for speed. The racing itself acts as speedwork.

One of the best "workouts" of this type is to race at about half your normal distance (for instance, a 10-K runner drops to 5-K). You run a little faster here than in your target race, which will make its pace seem a little easier to hold.

The racing schedule seldom meshes perfectly with your needs, however, so you may need supplemental speed training. One way to do this is with steady runs.

Run about half your upcoming race distance. Train—without walking or jogging breaks—at or near the expected pace of that race. The other—and very effective—way to increase speed is with interval training.

Intervals also total about half the race distance and again match race pace. But now you split that distance into segments and insert short walks of 1 to 5 minutes in between. For example, if your target race is the 1500, you'd interval train by running race pace, for 200 meters four times—four 200s—with walking in between.

The sample half-race, half-run, and half-interval workouts that follow are pegged to your target racing distance. Chapters 14 through 17 contain more programs to build speed for specific distances.

Target Race Distance	Half-Race or Half-Run	Half-Intervals
1500 m or 1 mi.	800 m	4 × 200 m
3000 m or 2 mi.	1500 m or 1 mi.	4 × 400 m
5 km	1500 m, 1 mi., or 2000 m	3 × 800 m
8 km	3000 m or 2 mi.	5 × 800 m
10 km	5000 m	3 × 1 mi.
15 km	5 km or 8 km	4 × 1 mi.
10 mi.	8 km or 5 km	5 × 1 mi.
20 km or half-marathon	10 km	6 × 1 mi.
15 mi. or 25 km	12 km	7 × 1 mi.
30 km	15 km	9 × 1 mi.
20 mi.	10 mi.	10 × 1 mi.
Marathon	20 km or half-marathon	13 × 1 mi.

year-round, but you should resist that temptation. Racing opportunities have spread throughout the year, but the old rules haven't changed. It's still a very rare runner who can race well indefinitely.

Your year needs a focus, a peak period or two. It also needs a rebuilding phase after each period of peaking.

Matching the highs and lows of racing to the seasons of the year also makes good sense for practical reasons. The best weather and most of the best races occur in spring and fall, and the least attractive racing comes in the coldest and hottest months.

Taper Your Training

David Costill, Ph.D., first made his name as an exercise physiologist two decades ago by studying runners at the now world-famous Human Performance Laboratory at Ball State University in Muncie, Indiana. His discoveries have changed the way runners race and train, eat and drink. Despite all this knowledge, Dr. Costill's own body betrayed him. In the early 1980s, running injuries sent him back to his original sport of swimming.

In his late forties, Dr. Costill soon was competing as a swimmer better than he had in college — not only better against men his age but better against the clock. "I was able to put to use some of the practical lessons learned from running and the laboratory," he says. "The main one is to train according to how I feel each day, judging when to push or back off."

Knowing how to work better and rest better is key to training. Dr. Costill says that "a final major factor in my second life as a swimmer is that I've learned a lot over the years about how to rest up for competition. In swimming, you can taper for up to three weeks by just warming up every day."

Dr. Costill's research indicates that runners also may need to taper up to three weeks before a major race in order to restore full bounciness to the legs, though race distances influence the period of reduced training. A 10-K runner, for example, might train hard within only one week of a big race, but a marathoner might schedule his last long run far in advance.

Of course, Dr. Costill doesn't expect you to train down weeks before every race, as a marathoner would, because that would leave a regular racer no time for anything but tapering. He does advise that you "reduce training and eat foods high in carbohydrates the last 72 hours" before most events.

Recover Right

Recovery after a race, explains Dr. Costill, is "tapering in reverse." Repay the fatigue debt with three days to three weeks of light training, and refuel the glycogen-starved legs with more carbos.

Recovery passes through three stages, two of which runners tend to ignore. The first stage is recovery from muscle stiffness and soreness. It lasts for a few days, and you aren't tempted to do much running in this condition.

You may think you're recovered when the legs loosen, but you're not. Two stages remain: recovery from fatigue and recovery of the mind.

Lingering tiredness—a vague feeling of dullness and heaviness when you run—often outlasts the muscular symptoms. Psychological recovery usually takes the longest. Olympic marathon champion Frank Shorter once said of this period, "You aren't ready to run another race until you forget how bad the last one felt."

The three-part recovery process is distance-related. You may get over a 5-K race in less than a week but feel the aftereffects of a marathon for a month or more.

The Jack Foster rule of one day of easy running or rest for each mile of the race serves the recovery needs of the youngest, best-trained runners. Many masters, however, might opt for a one-day-per-*kilometer* formula. (See "Race Spacing" on the opposite page.)

PW Priscilla on Peaking

Since early in my career, I've focused my attention on certain marathons. I've trained to win those marathons, be it the open or masters race.

If I've done the particular race before, like New York, London, or Boston, I know the course. I find terrain to train on that's as much like that course as possible.

I also choose shorter races that prepare me to peak for the marathon. Although I am serious about those races, I keep in mind that they are a means to an end and not an end in themselves. My focus remains on the marathon, not the shorter races.

I was most focused in 1987. To tell the truth, I haven't been highly focused since, but I'm working to regain that degree of focus.

I peaked twice in 1987. The first time was for the London Marathon in May. I wanted to run London really well because it had been the first marathon I'd trained properly for back in 1981. I also had this goal, going back to my first marathon of 3:26, to take a whole hour off that time. It was no longer unrealistic.

London's nice, fast course was the place to run a fast time. And this was a chance to prove myself in my home territory. I wanted to beat all the British girls and to break the national record.

I did a lot of the training for the London race in New Zealand. Then, six or

Race Spacing

As exciting and challenging as racing is, it also takes its toll. It leaves you tired and sore—and more vulnerable to illness and injury if you don't take enough time to recover.

Insure adequate recovery in the postrace period by observing the Jack Foster rule: Do no more hard running until one day has passed for each mile of the race.

Masters runners, who tend to recover slowly, might want to adopt a longer, one-day-per-*kilometer* period. You probably need at least an easy week after even the shortest races.

This table lists recommended recovery times in weeks for both miles and kilometers. Continue running during this period, but do no serious training or racing.

Race Distance	Recovery Time (wk.)	
	One Day per Mile	One Day per Kilometer
1500 m to 5 km	1	1
8 to 10 km	1	1½
12 km	1½	2
15 km and 10 mi.	1½	2½
20 km and half-marathon (13.1 mi.)	2	3
15 mi. and 25 km	2½	3½
30 km and 20 mi.	3	4½
Marathon (26.2 mi.)	4	6

seven weeks before the London Marathon I went to Japan to run the Nagoya Marathon. I finished in 2:38 off basework.

Everything in my preparation for London had been right. I felt happy with and confident in the training. I knew that I couldn't have done any more to prepare for a marathon. I know I can't have it my way all the time, but there are occasions when it all comes together, when it all clicks.

Only once before the start of a marathon have I felt light as a feather. That was London. Even during my warmup for the race, I knew that I was going to do something special. That's the day I ran 2:26:51. It was my best time by about 2 minutes, a British record, a world masters best, and exactly 1 hour faster than my first marathon!

Later in 1987, I focused again—this time on the New York City Marathon in November. Dave and I could see the doors partially open for a win there.

Some girls were backing off because of the Seoul Olympics the next year, so we decided to peak for New York.

The race director, Fred Lebow, didn't want to pay us any appearance money even after my good performance in London. I can remember being at the stove, cooking a meal, when Fred gave Dave that news over the telephone. As soon as Dave hung up the phone, he said to me, "You're going to win that sucker!" And I did, beating all the women in my best competitive effort.

I attribute my success in 1987 to proper peaking. But I've also seen the other side of peaking. After 1987, I wanted to do even better the next year at the Olympics in Seoul. But then I tried to do so much hard work to get an even better time that I went over the edge. I suffered stress fractures in both feet and learned a hard lesson.

Since then, it has been difficult to pick up again to the 1987 standard. I was very competitive in London and in New York, but I think I've relaxed that hungriness. That's what I've got to cultivate again—that hunger, that focus. ■

BR   Bill on Peaking

I love to race at any distance and at any time of year, so it may not seem that peaking is very important to me. But I focus on a few races, such as the Boston Marathon. I train more specifically for them than for the shorter distances.

I've always thought of myself primarily as a marathoner. Therefore, if I win or lose a 10-K it doesn't affect me as much as how I do in a marathon.

Until recently, top masters runners have tended to be generalists like me who run a wide variety of distances. But as the level of competition improves, we're seeing a trend toward specialization. Masters like Wilson Waigwa are best at the mile and 5-K. Bob Schlau is really a marathon specialist, though he also runs some shorter races.

Every successful runner—open or master, man or woman—has the ability to focus specifically on a certain big race. Of the runners I know, John Treacy does this best.

Treacy, a native of Ireland who now lives in the Boston area, is a two-time World Cross-Country champion. He won the silver medal in the 1984 Olympic Marathon—in his first race at that distance.

I sometimes train with Treacy, and I'm in awe of him. He knows how to train—not just how to train hard but also how to train intelligently. Plenty of people train hard, but many of them aren't very smart about taking rest or easy days.

One January, Treacy and I both ran a 10-K race in Charlotte, North

Carolina, and then flew directly to Phoenix for our winter training. Our first day in Phoenix, I was thinking, "Maybe I'll run twice today."

But no, Treacy knew that once was enough. He's as good about resting as he is about doing the hard training needed to peak for a certain race.

I think of peaking mostly as a matter of the training done before the event, because usually the race takes care of itself. The runners who race the best are those like Treacy who have the ability to focus well on their training. ■

13

Aiming to Win

Pacing and Other Tactics for Success

Bill and Priscilla won most of their fame in marathons and still think of themselves primarily as marathoners. Tactical skills play their greatest role at this distance.

Pacing is your *most* important tactic in any race, and never more so than in a marathon. At shorter distances, running the wrong pace slows your final time and knocks you down in the placings. In a marathon, this mistake can make the difference between finishing and not.

Your tactical weapons may include starting fast to escape your opponents right away, surging in midrace to break away from a challenger, or kicking at the finish to win an age-group prize. Yet your primary opponent is yourself, and your most important tactic is personal pacing.

Arthur Lydiard, a coach of Olympic champions from New Zealand who revolutionized distance training and racing methods in the 1960s, says that only the runners "fighting for championship honors" should concern themselves with racing each other. "Among them, attempts to break up the field are expected and warranted. But other runners are warned not to get tangled up in this sort of cutthroat running. They are the ones whose throat will be cut first."

Concern yourself first with running your own best race. That starts with knowing how fast you can expect to run. Then you start at that pace and focus on holding it.

Predictable Pace

Distance running is a predictable sport. You can look with some accuracy into your future by reviewing results from your recent past.

If you always raced the same distance, making these projections would be easy. But if you're like most distance runners, you compete at a wide variety of distances—a 5-K one week, a 10-K the next, and later a 20-K.

The rule of thumb for calculating your pace potential at different racing distances is to add 20 seconds per mile to your pace as the distance doubles, or to subtract that amount for a halving of the distance. For example, a 5-K runner who averages a 6:00 mile can expect to run about 6:20s for 10-K and 6:40s for 20-K.

Experienced runners and masters runners find this rule very useful. World-class athletes can cut or increase their pace by 17 seconds a mile.

For many masters runners, the 20-second rule may indeed apply, but it grows less reliable for those whose times are beginning to slow. A more accurate predictor of time is the Five Percent Rule.

Add 5 percent to your time at double the distance of your last race, or subtract 5 percent at half the distance. For example, say you recently ran 10 miles at a 7:30-per-mile pace. You can count on running your upcoming 5-mile race 5 percent faster, or at about a 7:08 pace. (See "Predicting Times" on pages 112 and 113 for comparable times for ten different racing distances.)

Though it can closely predict your final race time, the 5 percent formula gives you only a rough idea at what pace you'll finish. It best serves as an indicator of how fast you can safely *start* the race by basing your pacing plans on realistic expectations, not illusions.

Two-Part Pacing

Steady pace wins the race against time. Coach Lydiard refers to even-paced running as "the best way to get the best out of yourself."

The simplest way to judge even pace is to split the racing distance in half. The more equal the half-times are, the more efficient your pacing has been.

The current world record-holders in the open division ran more efficiently than any record-holder before them. Look how evenly they paced their halves. Miler Steve Cram ran his second half 3.5 seconds faster than his first. Marathoner Belaine Densimo's halves differed least, slowing by only 0.2 seconds per mile in his closing half. As a group, the record-holders deviated just 0.7 seconds from a perfectly even pace.

The lesson for you from the fastest and best-trained runners in the world is this: If you start faster than you finish, you lost considerably more speed in the

Predicting Times: The 5 Percent Solution

Before you can plan your race pace, you must know your racing potential. This need not be guesswork. Your most recent race time gives a good indication of what you can run in the next race, even when their distances differ.

Your performance at one distance can predict your potential at another if you use a simple formula. Masters runners typically slow down by about 5 percent as the race doubles in length—or speed up by that amount at half the distance.

For instance, a 7-minute-per-mile 5-K equates to a 7:21 pace for a 10-K. An 8-minute-paced marathon predicts a 7:36-per-mile half-marathon.

Using the 5 percent formula, this table lists comparable times for various racing distances. Times under an hour are rounded to the nearest half-minute, and those over an hour to the full minute.

Find your recent race result, then read across to your predicted time for an upcoming event. These comparisons work best when conditions are comparable. Extremes of weather and terrain may, of course, throw them off. After running the event, see how close your predictions come to your official time.

Compare these results to measure your training needs. Examples: A slower 10-K time than predicted based on your half-marathon time indicates a lack of speed. A slower marathon than anticipated based on your 15-K time means you may need to work on your endurance.

last half than you gained in the first. And if you drop too far behind an even pace in the first half, you can't make up that lost time in the second.

Run your half-times as equally as possible. In a well-paced race, these times shouldn't differ by more than 5 seconds per mile. (See "Pacing Plans" on page 115 for more on this "safety margin" at all the commonly raced distances.)

Running each half in equal time, however, doesn't mean they'll feel equal in effort. This style of pacing gives the sensation of accelerating all the way. You must hold back when you feel like breaking loose, and then push when you want to ease off.

This is the basic law of pacing. As Lydiard explained it to milers, "The best way to get full benefit of ability in the mile is to go out with the attitude that it is a ½-mile race, and the time to start putting on the pressure is when the first half-mile is behind you."

This pattern applies to all races. Start *cautiously,* not slowly but keeping

5-K	8-K/ 5-Mi.	10-K	12-K	15-K	10-Mi.	Half-Marathon	25-K	Marathon
15:00	25:00	31:00	37:30	47:30	52:00	1:09	1:23	2:25
15:30	25:30	32:00	39:00	49:00	53:30	1:11	1:26	2:29
16:00	26:30	33:00	40:00	50:30	55:30	1:13	1:29	2:33
16:30	27:00	34:00	41:00	52:00	57:00	1:15	1:31	2:38
17:00	28:00	35:00	42:30	54:00	59:00	1:18	1:34	2:43
17:30	29:00	36:00	43:30	55:30	1:00	1:20	1:37	2:48
18:00	30:00	37:00	45:00	57:00	1:02	1:22	1:39	2:52
18:30	30:30	38:00	46:00	58:30	1:04	1:24	1:42	2:56
19:00	31:30	39:00	47:30	1:00	1:06	1:26	1:45	3:01
19:30	32:00	40:00	48:30	1:02	1:08	1:29	1:48	3:06
20:00	33:00	41:00	49:30	1:03	1:09	1:31	1:51	3:11
20:30	34:00	42:00	51:00	1:05	1:11	1:33	1:53	3:15
21:00	34:30	43:00	52:00	1:06	1:13	1:35	1:56	3:20
21:30	35:30	44:00	53:30	1:08	1:14	1:37	1:58	3:24
22:00	36:00	45:00	54:30	1:09	1:16	1:40	2:01	3:29
22:30	37:00	46:00	56:00	1:11	1:18	1:42	2:04	3:34
23:00	38:00	47:00	57:00	1:12	1:20	1:44	2:06	3:38
23:30	39:00	48:00	58:00	1:14	1:21	1:46	2:09	3:42
24:00	39:30	49:00	59:30	1:15	1:23	1:49	2:12	3:48
24:30	40:30	50:00	1:01	1:17	1:25	1:51	2:14	3:53

speed in careful check. Then open up the reserve power systems after the halfway point.

Think of the race as two races, each the same in size but very different in style. Run the first half as a "pacer." Ignore the people around you who dash away from the starting line. Keep your head as they lose theirs.

Quietly set the stage for the point when real racing begins at about the halfway point. Now change styles. Run the second half as a "racer," with a competitive spirit. Pass the people who started their racing too soon and are starting to burn out.

Negative Splits

Racing the second half of a race faster than the first is a technique known as negative splits. Negative splits give positive results, says Don Kardong, who placed fourth for the United States in the 1976 Olympic Marathon and later won medals at the 1989 World Veterans Championships.

Kardong writes in *Runner's World* magazine that "negative splits may sound like a bad stretching technique." But, in fact, it means running the second half of a race faster than the first.

"It's an approach that few runners ever take," says Kardong. "Since most runners can't imagine that it's possible *not* to slow down late in a race, they run in a manner (going out too fast) that *guarantees* they will slow down.

"Yet it doesn't have to be that way. Running negative-split races may be one of the most powerful ways to improve your performances, particularly if you're stuck in a racing rut."

David Martin, Ph.D., of Georgia State University conducts physiological research on marathon runners for the U.S. Olympic Committee. He reports that a cautious start conserves glycogen and delays heat buildup in the muscles, thereby making a faster finish possible.

In one study, Dr. Martin compared the early and late race paces of world class marathoners. He found that those who ran the first 10 kilometers at a pace more than three percent faster than their average pace ended up running the last 10 kilometers more than five percent slower than their average pace. In essence, the faster they started, the slower they finished.

"On the other hand," says Dr. Martin, "the faster finishers consistently made their initial splits very close to or even slower than their overall pace."

Kardong comments, "It's very clear that the hardest part of any marathon is the final 10 kilometers or so. Holding physical and psychological reserves for this stage is essential. But the *perception* of negative splits at that point may be more important than the actual fact.

"In the final miles of the marathon, runners must work harder both physically and psychologically merely to hold pace. And that ends up feeling like negative splits. At the very least, a negative-split effort should give you that wonderful feeling of strength and power over the final miles of the race."

Leading researcher and coach Jack Daniels, Ph.D., whose tempo running we discussed in chapter 11, adds, "After the race, it's better to say you could have gone a little harder, a little earlier, than to wonder how much better you would have run if you hadn't killed yourself so soon."

BR Bill: "Know Your Foe"

You can't be swayed too much by other people's past results or what they do in the current race. You have to stick to your own goals and capabilities, and run your own race.

The ideal strategy is to run the best race *you* can on that day. Above all, you have to pace yourself.

As Juma Ikangaa demonstrated at the 1990 Boston Marathon (where he took the race out at world-record pace and then faded badly), even the number-

Pacing Plans

Your best pace is an even pace. That means saving enough early to allow a strong finish, but not starting so slowly that you can't make up the lost time later.

The two halves of the race should differ no more than 5 seconds per mile. To determine these safety margins, divide your projected time by two. Then add and subtract the appropriate amounts from the table to determine what your fastest and slowest halfway split should be.

For instance, your race distance is 10-K and your time goal is 40 minutes. The safety margin listed for this event is 31 seconds (6.2 miles times 5 seconds). So the first 5-K should pass no faster than 19:29 and no slower than 20:31, assuming that weather and hill conditions are comparable for both halves of the race.

After the race, compare times for the halves to see how close you came to even pace. If times differed by more than 5 seconds per mile, you raced inefficiently.

For more advice on pacing specific races, see chapters 14 (10-K), 15 (half-marathon), 16 (marathon), and 17 (track).

Race Distance	Halfway	Safety Margin
1500 km	750 km	0:04 sec.
1 mi.	0.5 mi.	0:05 sec.
3000 km	1500 km	0:09 sec.
2 mi.	1 mi.	0:10 sec.
5 km	2.5 km	0:16 sec.
8 km/5 mi.	4 km/2.5 mi.	0:25 sec.
10 km	5 km	0:31 sec.
12 km	6 km	0:38 sec.
15 km	7.5 km	0:47 sec.
10 mi.	5 mi.	0:50 sec.
20 km	10 km	1:02
Half-marathon (13.1 mi.)	6.55 mi.	1:05
25 km	12.5 km	1:17
30 km	15 km	1:33
20 mi.	10 mi.	1:40
Marathon (26.2 mi.)	13.1 mi.	2:35

one ranked marathon runner in the world can't pull off a suicidal pace from the start. No one can.

Running my own race doesn't mean that I ignore my competition. I always study who my competitors are and what their training and racing have been like leading up to the race. Sometimes this information warns me not to try and run at someone else's pace.

At the 1986 Boston Marathon, I knew that Rob de Castella would run very well. He towed the field out at an incredible pace, and most of the top runners tried to go with him.

I held back, as planned, and this tactic worked to my advantage. As we went along, I saw most of the top people coming back to me. I ended up placing fourth (and first American) at age 38.

When I reached 40, I began focusing on the masters. This was a smaller pond with fewer top competitors, so you can know them that much better. Part of my motivation now is knowing exactly who I have to compete against, whereas in open races I had to deal with the world.

Despite my efforts to know the competition, some of the new people entering my age group still catch me by surprise. Dave Stewart from Canada did this at the 1989 ICI Championships when he finished second. I didn't have a clue who he was, and even though I won by a big margin I wanted to know more about him.

The next time we raced, at a Canadian 10-K in May 1989, he beat me when I was a little injured. After recovering, I beat him at the Charlotte 10-K in January 1990. Now that I know Stewart, I also know where I stand against him.

But knowing your competitors isn't always enough. You need to be able to identify them, too. This can be a problem in the crowded open races where all the age groups run together.

At the 1988 Los Angeles Marathon, I was confident of winning the masters title. I started that race conservatively and thought 2:23 to 2:25 would win it.

A New Zealander had gone out in 2:22 pace, but I was able to reel him in by 15 miles. I thought I'd taken the lead for masters, then my brother Charlie told me that Bob Schlau was still ahead by about a minute.

I tried to catch Schlau but never saw him. I lost him in the crowd. Keeping an eye on the competition is difficult for masters runners. Race directors should realize this and start putting numbers on our backs that indicate our age group. Without proper identification, it makes monitoring your progress almost impossible. How are you supposed to know that the guy 300 yards ahead of you is competing against you? ■

Pw Priscilla: "Concentrate"

When I first came to the United States, I got caught up in all the razzmatazz of races. It was all new to me, and I used to take in all the events.

I used up a lot of energy that way. Now I usually just go to my room and rest up for the race.

I concentrate on the job at hand. The other masters women are improving now, and I'm more vulnerable. I can't afford to take any race lightly.

One of my strengths, I think, is an ability to concentrate. I specialize in marathons, and 26 miles is a long way to stay focused.

For my two big marathons of 1987, London and New York City, I concentrated extremely well.

In London, I said to myself after hearing the 10-kilometer time, "Ooh, that's a bit fast! How do I feel? Okay. Concentrate!" I talked to myself the same way at 10 miles, the half-marathon, and so on.

New York was a different type of race. In London, I didn't really expect to beat world record-holder Ingrid Kristiansen (who was indeed the winner that day) and was running for a fast time.

In New York, I was running to win in whatever time it took. Contrary to the usual advice to start out easy, my tactic was to go like mad from the start until 8 miles, where the women's field converged with the men's and it became difficult for women who weren't running together to find each other in the crowded field.

I wanted to make sure I was well enough ahead that no one could run off me. Laura Fogli of Italy was still with me at 8 miles, but having her there for a while didn't shake my concentration.

I held my focus that day until we entered Central Park near the finish. I lost it a wee bit there and started slowing down, in part because I was tiring and in part because of all the official vehicles hovering about.

When you're running first, you face lots of distractions. A motorbike nearly hit me. But I regained my focus by telling myself, "I've come this far in the lead, and no one is going to beat me over the line."

Kim Jones said that at the 1989 New York City Marathon, where she placed second, she didn't concern herself too much with who else was in the field. I know what she was trying to say, because I run most of my races as she did there.

You can't totally ignore the field. You have to know where you stand, as Bill Rodgers says.

But mainly you need to have confidence in the training you've done. You've got to know your own capabilities and not try to run someone else's race. You have to run your own best pace and not let anyone set it for you.

If I were Ingrid Kristiansen, Grete Waitz, Rosa Mota, or Joan Benoit Samuelson, I would probably use more sophisticated tactics for a marathon. But I'm not in their class, really. I haven't refined my act as much as they have.

With rare exceptions like New York and London in 1987, I'm not racing the marathon for the win or to set records like those girls are. I'm trying to get the best out of me on that particular day. I have come to a realistic conclusion about what I can do, and I simply concentrate on doing it.

I seldom feel nervous before races, especially 10-K races. When I told Ingrid Kristiansen about approaching my events rather calmly, she was amazed. "I feel very, very nervous—almost to the point of being sick," she said.

I told her, "You're in a different league than I am. You're a gal who likes to go for medals and records, and *can* go for them. I'm just running to do the best I can."

Perhaps another reason that I'm not so nervous about races is that I'm older and have had quite a few other things in my life to worry about. By comparison, racing is a pleasant diversion. ■

14

Conquering the 10-K

Advice for Short Road Runs

While Priscilla and Bill have raced their best at the marathon distance, they have done the *most* racing in the 10-K range (5-K through 12-K). Almost everyone does, because most road races fall into this range—the shorter distances that take most runners less than an hour to complete.

A strong case can be made for the 10-K (6.2 miles) and its companions being the perfect racing distances. The primary appeal of these distances is their close resemblance to everyday running. Training runs typically settle into a half-hour to an hour, the same amount of time needed to finish most short races. Therefore, the distance isn't too long.

And because the race distance isn't too short, the pace is manageable. The challenge of racing these distances lies in running that familiar distance faster than normal, but not recklessly fast. This is not a mad dash the way a single all-out mile might be.

Yet races in this range are truly raced. They differ from marathons, which for the bulk of runners are survival tests taken slower than training pace.

Training for better racing in the 10-K range can be as simple as modestly increasing the pace of one or two runs each week (see "10-K Plans" on page 121). Little or no special attention needs be paid to long runs, because normal daily training usually supplies all the length required for these races.

Runners who enjoy racing want to race often. The 10-K and similar races allow this because recovery occurs quickly. Applying the standard formula of one easy day following each racing mile, you can safely run these races as often as every week, though it would leave little room to train for a peak performance since you would only have time to recover and race, recover and race.

The 10-K range serves as a meeting place for the greatest number and widest variety of runners. Eight of the ten largest U.S. races come from this range, and each draws an average of 30,000 entrants. First-time racers start alongside world-class competitors. Marathoners race against track athletes. Masters run with the young stars.

Welch holds the masters women 10-K world best, with 32:14. Rodgers is the fastest American master (though not the official record-holder), with 29:48.

Pw Priscilla on 10-K's

My record 10-K surprised me. I wasn't specifically trained for that distance at the time of the 1985 Azalea Run in Mobile, Alabama. But I had run a lot of short races, and they had honed my speed to its sharpest point ever. I'd already lowered the world masters 10-K record twice within the past two months, to 32:41 and then 32:25.

What I remember most about the race in Mobile was how hungry I felt to win the race overall. In the later stages, Linda McLennan (now Begley) was on my shoulder and the crowd was yelling, "Come on, Linda!"

I thought surely she couldn't be with me. But she was, and we had just the finishing straight left. No way was she going to beat me, and she didn't. But she improved her PR by almost a minute to 32:19.

I ran 32:14. At this writing, the time still stands as a world masters record and my personal best.

To break it, I would need to train specifically for this distance. A 10-K is about 90 percent aerobic—meaning you're running at 90 percent of your total aerobic capacity. (A marathon is probably 98 percent aerobic.) You've got to develop the aerobic system and the capacity to burn fat for the 10-K. But that's not quite as important for the shorter distance as it is for the marathon.

What's more important in the 10-K is being able to run very fast at your aerobic/anaerobic threshold—that is, the fastest pace you can maintain within your aerobic capacity. You've got to train for speed in the 10-K.

There are women marathoners who can break 2:30 but can't run under 34 minutes for 10-K. They need more speedwork. (My best marathon was 2:28:54 at the time I ran the 32:14 10-K.)

They might want to do some interval training like 20 runs of 400 meters on a track at a steady pace, slightly slower than 10-K race pace, with a very short interval—maybe only 10 to 15 seconds in between. (Interval training is dis-

10-K Plans

You're preparing for a big 10-K a few weeks away. You're in good general shape now but want to sharpen up a little more for that race.

Start by deemphasizing distance. Limit your long runs to an hour, and put the effort you save there into extra speedwork.

Schedule two fast sessions each week: one as intervals, and the other either a tempo run, a shorter race, or the 10-K itself. (See chapters 11 and 12 for detailed advice on training and racing fast.)

A sample weekly plan follows. You might work up to a 10-K peak in three weeks with a 5-K tempo run the first weekend, a 5-K race the second, and then the 10-K.

This is labeled a 10-K program, but you can adapt it for other short road races by tailoring the length of speed runs to the racing distance.

Day	Plan
1	Optional day: easy run, cross-training, or rest
2	Long run: 1 hour at much slower than race pace
3	Optional day: easy run, cross-training, or rest
4	Intervals: 3 times 1 mile at about 10-K race pace, *or* optional day the week of the big 10-K race
5	Optional day: easy run, cross-training, or rest
6	Big day: 5-K tempo run at about 10-K race pace, *or* 5-K race at close to top speed, *or* 10-K race at top speed
7	Optional day: easy run, cross-training, or rest

cussed in chapter 12.) Another session might be anaerobic threshold training: 6 to 8 runs lasting 3 to 6 minutes each, with a 2-minute recovery between.

If you want to improve your short-distance racing, you have to train for those distances. You can't be training for them and the marathon at the same time.

You also must decide exactly what your purpose is. Are you training for optimal performance, or do you want to race every weekend of the year?

If you're going to do the latter, then you'll be more content with a complex training schedule that combines all the ingredients: some aerobic work, running comfortably within your aerobic capacity; some threshold work, running at the fastest pace you can maintain without becoming anaerobic; and some strength work such as hill training. It will keep you in all-around good shape all the time.

In England's harrier clubs, there's a tendency to train the same the whole year through and also to race year-round. The trouble with this system is that

The 10-K Time Challenge

A family of races surrounds the 10-K. Distances from 5-K to 12-K all require similar training and tactics.

This table lists comparable times for these short road races. It is based on the 5 percent formula: As the distance doubles, runners typically slow by 5 percent—or speed up by that amount at half the distance.

Times here are rounded to the nearest 15 seconds. Refer to your most recent race time in the table to find your *predicted* time for your upcoming race. If you raced a 15:15 5-K, for example, you can predict a 32:00 10-K.

10-K	5-K	8-K	12-K
30:00	14:15	23:30	36:30
31:00	14:45	24:15	37:45
32:00	15:15	25:00	39:00
33:00	15:45	25:45	40:15
34:00	16:15	26:30	41:30
35:00	16:45	27:15	42:45
36:00	17:15	28:00	44:00
37:00	17:30	29:00	45:15
38:00	18:00	29:45	46:15
39:00	18:30	30:30	47:30
40:00	19:00	31:15	48:45
41:00	19:30	32:00	50:00
42:00	20:00	32:45	51:15
43:00	20:30	33:30	52:30
44:00	21:00	34:15	53:45
45:00	21:30	35:15	55:00
46:00	22:00	36:00	56:00
47:00	22:30	36:45	57:15
48:00	22:45	37:30	58:30
49:00	23:15	38:15	59:45
50:00	23:45	39:00	1:01:00
51:00	24:15	39:45	1:02:15
52:00	24:45	40:30	1:03:30
53:00	25:15	41:30	1:04:45
54:00	25:45	42:15	1:06:00
55:00	26:15	43:00	1:07:00
56:00	26:45	43:45	1:08:15
57:00	27:15	44:30	1:09:30
58:00	27:30	45:15	1:10:45
59:00	28:00	46:00	1:12:00

you rarely reach peak performance, or if you do you can't predict when it will come.

If you train for peak performance, you want to hit it at the designated time. If you want to do well in the shorter road races, you've got to train for a specific racing season lasting six to eight weeks and to peak at that time.

You may be able to squeeze in two of these peak periods a year—say, one in the spring and another in the fall. But I've done best by just peaking once in a year.

Ideally, if I were attempting to peak in late summer, I would start to build an aerobic base in October and November. I'd begin to add threshold training and speedwork around February, approach the peak in June, and run my best races in July and August. Then I'd rest for a few weeks before starting the cycle again.

That's how you reach peak performance. You periodize your training to build up for a particular racing season.

When you plan this way, you've got to factor in time off for injuries as well. I know it's not a good thing to think "injury" even before you start training. But you do have to throw in an extra two or three weeks as time to recuperate and still save your season.

One of the best ways to improve your speed during the racing season is to run shorter-than-normal races. It would do me a world of good to run more 5-K's when I'm preparing for a 10-K.

I suggest that you start off the season with a 5-K and then move up in distance. In Norway, where I did my earliest racing, the season begins in April with a lot of 5-K's. The distances then increase to 8-K and 10-K as the runners get fitter. Everybody builds up together. ■

BR Bill on 10-K's

This book opened by describing my overall victory at the 1988 Heartland Hustle 10-K as a 40-year-old. The fact is, the field wasn't very strong that year and I was on my own by the 2-mile mark.

I was running for time, trying to get under Barry Brown's American masters record of 29:57. The humid but cool day was conducive to a good time, and the out-and-back course was fast and flat. I broke the record by 9 seconds, but the paperwork for approving the mark has never been completed.

I'm proud of my short-distance records because I've always thought of myself as a marathoner who is a little bit out of his element in these events. But I still compete pretty well with the speedsters.

I never needed a muscle biopsy to tell me that I'm not built for speed, and I've never aimed for distances shorter than 10-K. Even in high school and

(continued on page 126)

Masters 10-K Records

Care to know how your times for this distance compare with those of the best runners in your age-group? Check the world and American records for your group.

National Masters News publishes the best track times in its annual booklet titled *Masters Age Records*. (To order a booklet, write to NMN, Box 16597, North Hollywood, CA 91615.)

The Athlete's Congress Statistics (TACSTATS) maintains road running records for the Athletics Congress at all the commonly run distances — including the 5-K, 8-K, and 12-K covered in this chapter. (For a current listing, contact TACSTATS at 915 Randolph, Santa Barbara, CA 93111.) These are the fastest times on courses that meet TAC's exacting standards for layout, certification, and validation.

Here, we list world 10,000-meter records only from the track because international road courses aren't often measured as carefully as those in the United States. We include both the American track (noted with a "t") and road ("r") 10-K marks.

These are the records approved through the end of 1990. (An * indicates the fastest pending road time in age-groups with no ratified record.) Track marks are accepted in hundredths of a second for automatic timing and tenths for hand timing. Road times are rounded up to the next full second for record purposes.

Men's World Records

Age	Name (Country)	Time
40–44	Lucien Rault (France)	28:33.4
45–49	Antonio Villanueva (Mexico)	30:02.56
50–54	Edgar Friedli (Switzerland)	31:51.29
55–59	Gunther Hesselmann (W. Germany)	32:50.3
60–64	John Gilmour (Australia)	34:23.0
65–69	Thedde Jensen (Sweden)	36:04.6
70–74	John Gilmour	38:27.0
75–79	David Morrison (Britain)	42:03.4
80–84	Ed Benham (U.S.)	42:38.79
85–89	Josef Galia (W. Germany)	54:23.0
90–94	Paul Spangler (U.S.)	71:40.78

Women's World Records

Age	Name (Country)	Time
40–44	Evy Palm (Sweden)	32:47.25
45–49	Evy Palm	32:41.98
50–54	Edeltraud Pohl (W. Germany)	36:51.6
55–59	Jean Albury (Australia)	38:38.6
60–64	Joselyn Ross (Britain)	43:01.2
65–69	Jose Waller (Britain)	46:52.2
70–74	Pat Dixon (U.S.)	50:28.33
75–79	Johanna Luther (W. Germany)	53:20.50
80–84	Hilda Crooks (U.S.)	1:38:38.0

Men's American Records

Age	Name	Time
40–44r	Barry Brown	29:57
40–44t	Larry Almberg	30:50.37
45–49r	Sal Vasquez	31:06
45–49t	Ray Hatton	31:48.0
50–54r	Ray Hatton	31:48
50–54t	Ray Hatton	32:10.4
55–59r	Norm Green	33:20
55–59t	Norm Green	33:00.66
60–64r	Jim O'Neil	34:27
60–64t	Clive Davies	35:19.8
65–69r*	Clive Davies	35:52
65–69t	Norman Bright	38:38.0
70–74r	Alfred Funk	41:09
70–74t	Ray Sears	41:21.0
75–79r	Ed Benham	43:24
75–79t	Ed Benham	43:54.75
80–84r	Ed Benham	45:28
80–84t	Ed Benham	44:29.4
85–89r	Paul Spangler	58:50
85–89t	Paul Spangler	1:03:58.4
90–94r	None	
90–94t	Paul Spangler	71:40.78

(continued)

Masters 10-K Records—*Continued*

Women's American Records

Age	Name	Time
40–44r	Gabriele Andersen	34:32
40–44t	Laurie Binder	35:20.59
45–49r	Joan Colman	36:19
45–49t	Vicky Bigelow	38:19.8
50–54r	Marion Irvine	37:43
50–54t	Mila Kania	38:53.6
55–59r*	Margaret Miller	39:59
55–59t	Marion Irvine	40:37.13
60–64r	Helen Dick	43:55
60–64t	Pat Dixon	44:51.0
65–69r	Helen Dick	47:16
65–69t	Jaclyn Caselli	49:22.41
70–74r	Algene Williams	54:23
70–74t	Pat Dixon	50:28.33
75–79r*	Leona Lugers	53:08
75–79t	Pearl Mehl	1:04:00.81
80–84r*	Leona Lugers	56:14
80–84t	Hilda Crooks	1:38:38.0

college, I was more suited for the longer races, and in my whole career I've only run one 5000 on the track.

Having said this, I quickly add that even a marathoner needs to get away from marathon training for a portion of the year. I used to train for the marathon year-round but now escape it during the summer.

This time of year, I don't do as much mileage and certainly let the distance of the long runs slip. Instead of running for 2 to 2½ hours, I run a little over 1½ hours as my longest run of the week.

You have to make concessions somewhere if you're focusing on the shorter races. Usually, I find that it's best to reduce the long run that is the most fatiguing, particularly for masters runners.

When I make this reduction, my legs are fresher and more effective in speedwork. I'm capable of reaching a higher level of quality in my training and can focus better on the shorter races. If I'm training for every distance from 5-K to the marathon, it's a grind.

One particular workout that helps me train for the shorter events is hill repeats. Where I now live in the Boston area, there's a 1500-meter section of road that is half-dirt, half-asphalt. It's mainly flat, but there are some rolling

10-K Pacing

An evenly paced 10-K is the ideal, but the pace need not be perfectly even. Times for the two halves of the race can vary by as much as 5 seconds per mile—31 seconds total for a 10-K—without hurting your result. But if the spread grows wider, you suffer.

The table below lists the fastest and slowest recommended halfway splits at various 10-K speeds. Find your predicted final time (see "The 10-K Time Challenge" on page 122), then plan to run each half of the race within the range of maximum splits listed.

After the race, analyze your time by subtracting the faster half from the slower. If they differ by more than 31 seconds, plan to adjust your starting pace the next time you run this distance.

Maximum differences for splits in other short road races are 16 seconds for 5-K, 25 seconds for 8-K, and 38 seconds for 12-K.

10-K	Even 5-K'S	Maximum Splits
30:00	15:00	14:45–15:16
31:00	15:30	15:15–15:46
32:00	16:00	15:45–16:16
33:00	16:30	16:15–16:46
34:00	17:00	16:45–17:16
35:00	17:30	17:15–17:46
36:00	18:00	17:45–18:16
37:00	18:30	18:15–18:46
38:00	19:00	18:45–19:16
39:00	19:30	19:15–19:46
40:00	20:00	19:45–20:16
41:00	20:30	20:15–20:46
42:00	21:00	20:45–21:16
43:00	21:30	21:15–21:46
44:00	22:00	21:45–22:16
45:00	22:30	22:15–22:46
46:00	23:00	22:45–23:16
47:00	23:30	23:15–23:46
48:00	24:00	23:45–24:16
49:00	24:30	24:15–24:46
50:00	25:00	24:45–25:16
51:00	25:30	25:15–25:46
52:00	26:00	25:45–26:16
53:00	26:30	26:15–26:46
54:00	27:00	26:45–27:16
55:00	27:30	27:15–27:46
56:00	28:00	27:45–28:16
57:00	28:30	28:15–28:46
58:00	29:00	28:45–29:16

hills that make it tough. I'll do six 1500 meters on this road.

I do much of my anaerobic training on the road. Another workout is 400s where I estimate my time because I don't know the exact distance. Sometimes, though, I need to go to the track to sharpen my sense of pace.

You have to know how a certain pace feels, what is fast enough and what's too fast. Everyone should realize that even the top runners in the world often go out too fast in a race. It makes sense always to err on the side of caution.

It also makes sense—even if you're running a 5-K to 12-K—to respect the heat. Because the distance is short, you may think you can get by with going out too hard and not taking enough water on a hot day. But I've seen lots of people go down in 5-K's.

Look what happened to Alberto Salazar at the 7-mile Falmouth Road Race in 1978. He collapsed from heat exhaustion after the race and had to be packed in ice to bring his body temperature down. No one is immune from severe dehydration. ■

15

The Half-Marathon Challenge

A Training Plan for Midrange Road Races

Few runners specialize in middle-distance road races—15-K to 25-K. But these distances have helped both Priscilla and Bill to prepare for their specialty—the marathon. And if marathoning is your goal, these races could help you, too.

Bill ran a record 30-K (18.6 miles) shortly before winning his first Boston Marathon in 1975. Before Priscilla's biggest victory, at the 1987 New York City Marathon, she won a 15-mile race that she fit into her schedule as a major test of her fitness.

The middle distances take about 1 to 2 hours to complete. For Bill and Priscilla, this range would extend from 20-K (12.4 miles) to 20 miles. For you, it's more likely to be 15-K (9.3 miles) to 25-K (15.5 miles). These distances surround the half-marathon—a race somewhat hard to find but well worth the search.

Half Measures

Our purpose here is to sell you on the hidden beauties of a perfectly lovely event. We like everything about it except its name, "half-marathon."

This makes it sound like a low-rent marathon, a discount item. And it's often treated as the second-class event at marathons, added for people who can't or won't put out a full marathon effort.

Runners in the "half" are also misled by its name. They think that doubling their half-marathon time indicates their marathon potential. They think, "If I ran my half in 1:45, I must now be ready for 3:30 at the full distance."

But think about it. No one expects Sebastian Coe to run twice as far at his world-record 800-meter pace to break the now-standing 3:46 mile. If he did, he'd run a 3:24! Yet we mistakenly assume that a road runner should be able to maintain a half-marathon pace for another 13.1 miles.

If that were possible, American masters half-marathon record-holder Barry Brown would be a 2:12 marathoner instead of a 2:15 man. Barbara Filutze, who holds the U.S. women's mark for the half, would be running marathons in the 2:32 range instead of about 10 minutes slower.

The typical conversion formula between the two distances for runners equal to Brown's and Filutze's ability is to double the half-marathon time and *add* about 5 minutes. But here we fall into the very trap we wanted to avoid. We, too, cheapen the half by comparing it to the marathon.

The beauty of the half-marathon is that it's a unique event, with its own special training and pacing requirements—and its own rewards. Don't sell it short just because it isn't as popular as either the marathon or the 10-K.

The fact that it's unpopular is one of this race's main attractions, since it doesn't usually bring out the crowds of either the 10-K or the marathon. Very few half-marathons attract more than 1,000 runners, and smallness may be an attraction after you've fought your way through a few mob scenes.

The half should also attract you for a number of other reasons.

• It is the least-tapped source of personal records. The less often you have raced the 15-K, 10-mile, 20-K, or half-marathon, the easier it should be to set a PR.

• It combines speed and endurance better than either the shorter or longer events. Ten-K training heavily emphasizes speed at the expense of distance, while marathon training leans heavily toward distance at the expense of speed. Half-marathon training blends modest amounts of both elements. (See "Half-Marathon Plans" on the opposite page.)

• It isn't so fast that it requires a great deal of speedwork like the shorter races do.

• Distance isn't so great that it demands extra-long training runs. Two hours is the longest time you need to train.

• No "wall" is likely to loom between you and the finish line. And when you don't hit a wall, you can race faster and recover more quickly afterward.

BR Bill on Middle Distances

Two of my proudest moments as a runner concern events that almost no one remembers. Both were record-setting races on the track in the 1970s.

Half-Marathon Plans

Training for the half-marathon blends the training requirements of the 10-K and the marathon. The in-between race demands less speed than the shorter one but more than the longer one, and vice versa in terms of distance. You can take fewer speed workouts before a half-marathon than a 10-K, and more long runs than before a marathon (because the distances and recovery times are less).

Schedule one long run, one medium-length run (about half as far as the long run), and one fast run each week. Work the long runs up to the projected time of your half-marathon. Work tempo runs of up to 10-K, intervals of up to six times a mile, and races of up to 10-K.

A sample weekly program follows. While it applies to the half-marathon, you can adjust the pace and distance to any of middle-distance road races—those lasting 1 to 2 hours, or about 15-K to 25-K.

Day	Plan
1	Medium run: half of long-run time, slower than race
2	Optional day: easy run, cross-training, or rest
3	Long run: work up to half-marathon time, slower than race
4	Optional day: easy run, cross-training, or rest
5	Optional day: easy run, cross-training, or rest
6	Big day: up to 10-K tempo run at about half-marathon race pace
	Intervals: up to 6 times a mile at about half-marathon race pace, *or* up to 10-K race at close to top speed, *or* half-marathon race at top speed
7	Optional day: easy run, cross-training, or rest

I've always been a record-conscious runner. In 1977, I set out to break the world record for the 1-hour run.

This may sound like an odd race, seeing how far you can run in an hour. But the world mark is officially recognized, and it's a great competitive event that has been attempted by many of the biggest names in the sport.

Jos Hermens of the Netherlands set the world record of 20,944 meters (a shade over 13 miles) in 1976. The next year, I tried to better that record.

I knew I could never get a world record for 10,000 meters, because my best time was 28:04, about 40 seconds off that mark. But I thought I had a shot at the 1-hour and went for it on the Boston University track.

I set the American record with 20,547 meters but missed Hermens' distance by a little less than a lap. He still holds the world record today.

The Half-Marathon Time Challenge

A family of races surrounds the half-marathon. Distances from 15-K to 25-K (9.3 to 15.5 miles) all require similar training and tactics.

This table lists comparable times for some of the middle-distance road races. It is based on the 5 percent formula explained in chapter 13. As the distance doubles, runners typically slow by 5 percent—or speed up by that amount at half the distance. (See "Predictable Pace" on page 111.)

Refer to your most recent race time in the table to find your *predicted* time for your upcoming race. If you raced a 48:30 15-K, for example, you can predict a 1:10 half-marathon. Times here are rounded to the nearest half-minute.

Half-Marathon	15-K	10-Mile	20-K
1:06:00	45:30	49:30	1:02:30
1:08:00	47:00	50:30	1:04:00
1:10:00	48:30	52:00	1:06:00
1:12:00	49:30	53:30	1:08:00
1:14:00	51:30	55:00	1:10:00
1:16:00	52:30	56:30	1:11:30
1:18:00	54:00	58:00	1:13:30
1:20:00	55:00	59:30	1:15:30
1:22:00	56:30	1:01:00	1:17:30
1:24:00	58:00	1:02:30	1:19:00
1:26:00	59:30	1:04:00	1:21:00
1:28:00	1:00:30	1:05:30	1:23:00
1:30:00	1:02:00	1:07:00	1:25:00
1:32:00	1:03:30	1:08:30	1:27:00
1:34:00	1:05:00	1:10:00	1:28:30
1:36:00	1:06:00	1:11:30	1:30:30
1:38:00	1:07:30	1:13:00	1:32:30
1:40:00	1:09:00	1:14:30	1:34:30
1:42:00	1:10:30	1:16:00	1:36:00
1:44:00	1:11:30	1:17:30	1:38:00
1:46:00	1:13:00	1:19:00	1:40:00
1:48:00	1:14:30	1:20:30	1:42:00
1:50:00	1:16:00	1:22:00	1:44:00
1:52:00	1:17:00	1:23:30	1:45:30
1:54:00	1:18:30	1:25:00	1:47:30
1:56:00	1:20:00	1:26:30	1:49:30
1:58:00	1:21:30	1:28:00	1:51:30
2:00:00	1:23:00	1:29:30	1:53:00
2:02:00	1:24:00	1:31:00	1:55:00
2:04:00	1:25:30	1:32:30	1:57:00
2:06:00	1:27:00	1:34:00	1:59:00
2:08:00	1:28:30	1:35:30	2:01:00

Later, I met Pekka Paivarinta, a Finn who had won the World Cross-Country title in 1973 and holds the track record for 25-K with 1:14:17. We were at a banquet at the Fukuoka (Japan) Marathon in 1977, and he didn't speak much English. He stood up and introduced himself with the description, "World record!" He wasn't bragging but just identifying himself by what he had done.

Dave Prokop, an employee of *Runner's World* magazine, directed my assault on Paivarinta's record in February 1979. After I hit Paivarinta's 25-K mark, I would then continue running to 30-K in an attempt to set an American record at that distance. We scheduled this race at a junior college track in Saratoga, California.

I left the other runners behind early, and from there on, ran against the clock. Timers gave me splits every lap, and I was always within a couple of seconds of world-record pace.

When I passed 25-K, the timers didn't tell me my time. I had to run another lap before learning that I had broken the record by 6 seconds with 1:14:11.8. I finished the 30-K in American-record time of 1:31:49.0.

Toshihiko Seko of Japan broke my 25-K world record two years later with 1:13:55, but both my 25-K and 30-K times still stand as American records more than ten years after I set them.

I still think the 25-K and 30-K are great distances. But it's tough to find races at these distances, or even a good half-marathon. These distances don't carry as much glamour as the 10-K and marathon.

I also like the 15-K. These races are hard and competitive like the 10-K, but they don't leave you annihilated as the marathon does. ■

PW Priscilla on Middle Distances

As you know, 1987 was my banner year in the marathon. That fall, I was pointing all my efforts toward the New York City race in November.

One of my key tests was the Charleston (West Virginia) Distance run on Labor Day weekend, almost exactly two months before New York. The Charleston race is 15 miles. Begun in the early 1970s, it has a proud tradition as one of the country's earliest races with invited stars.

I didn't wait for an invitation to arrive; Dave and I requested one from the race organizers in Charleston. It was one of the few races I could find at this distance, and it fit perfectly into my plans. I wanted to test myself at a distance more demanding than the 10-K but less taxing than the full marathon. At 15 miles, Charleston was ideal.

My first goal there was to win the women's race overall. My second ambition was to break the course record. That mark wasn't any soft touch, because Grete Waitz held it. Earlier, she had sought out the Charleston for the same marathon-preparation purpose that I did.

Half-Marathon Pacing

An evenly paced half-marathon is your ideal. But times for each 6.55 miles of the race can vary by as much as 5 seconds per mile—66 seconds total—without hurting your result.

The table below lists the fastest and slowest recommended 6.55-mile splits at various half-marathon speeds. Find your predicted final time (see "The Half-Marathon Time Challenge" on page 132), then plan to run each 6.55 miles within the range of maximum splits listed.

After the race, analyze your time by subtracting the faster 6.55-mile time from the slower. If they differ by more than 66 seconds, plan to adjust your starting pace the next time you run this distance.

Maximum differences for splits in other middle-distance road races are 47 seconds for 15-K, 50 seconds for 10 miles, 62 seconds for 20-K, and 77 seconds for 25-K.

Half-Marathon	Even 6.55-Miles	Maximum Splits
1:06:00	33:00	32:27–33:33
1:08:00	34:00	33:27–34:33
1:10:00	35:00	34:27–35:33
1:12:00	36:00	35:27–36:33
1:14:00	37:00	36:27–37:33
1:16:00	38:00	37:27–38:33
1:18:00	39:00	38:27–39:33
1:20:00	40:00	39:27–40:33
1:22:00	41:00	40:27–41:33
1:24:00	42:00	41:27–42:33
1:26:00	43:00	42:27–43:33
1:28:00	44:00	43:27–44:33
1:30:00	45:00	44:27–45:33
1:32:00	46:00	45:27–46:33
1:34:00	47:00	46:27–47:33
1:36:00	48:00	47:27–48:33
1:38:00	49:00	48:27–49:33
1:40:00	50:00	49:27–50:33
1:42:00	51:00	50:27–51:33
1:44:00	52:00	51:27–52:33
1:46:00	53:00	52:27–53:33
1:48:00	54:00	53:27–54:33
1:50:00	55:00	54:27–55:33
1:52:00	56:00	55:27–56:33
1:54:00	57:00	56:27–57:33
1:56:00	58:00	57:27–58:33
1:58:00	59:00	58:27–59:33
2:00:00	1:00:00	59:27–1:00:33
2:02:00	1:01:00	1:00:27–1:01:33
2:04:00	1:02:00	1:01:27–1:02:33
2:06:00	1:03:00	1:02:27–1:03:33
2:08:00	1:04:00	1:03:27–1:04:33

I entered the stadium for a final lap around the track, leading all the women. Dave shouted at me that I had a shot at the record if I sprinted hard to the finish. I did and broke Grete's course mark by 6 seconds with 1:24:52.

I wish there were more racing opportunities at this distance. The 8-, 10-, 12-, and 15-K's at one end of the spectrum and the marathons at the other draw most of the money, publicity, and crowds. Little is left over for the distances in between.

There is a smattering of activity in the half-marathon. But the next 13 miles might as well be known as the "black hole of running." The sport needs another popular race between the half-marathon and marathon. I nominate the 15 miles or 25-K, which stands almost exactly between the 10-K and marathon. (Chapter 16 contains more advice on running the 15-mile or 25-K distance.) ■

Masters Half-Marathon Records

You can compare your half-marathon time with that of the country's best runners in your age-group. No official organizations keep world records for this road race.

But in the United States, The Athlete's Congress Statistics (TACSTATS) maintains American records for all the commonly run distances — 15-K, 10 miles, 20-K, and 25-K. To request a current listing, write to TACSTATS, 915 Randolph, Santa Barbara, CA 93111. These are the fastest times on courses that meet TAC's exacting standards for layout, certification, and validation.

In the absence of world half-marathon records, we offer the world's best times for the 1-hour run on the track, which is officially measured in miles (mi.) and yards (yd.). *National Masters News* compiles these marks. For more information, write Box 16597, North Hollywood, CA 91615.

Here are the masters age-group records approved through early 1991. (An * indicates the fastest pending road time in age-groups with no ratified record.)

Women's American Records

Age	Name	Time
40–44	Barbara Filutze	1:16:00
45–49	Dorothy Stock	1:24:07
50–54	Marion Irvine	1:23:16
55–59	Margaret Miller	1:28:42
60–64	Helen Dick	1:39:01
65–69	Margaret Wright	1:58:31
70–74	Marcie Trent	1:58:27
75–79	Anne Clarke	2:26:24
80–84*	Ruth Rothfarb	2:30:41
85–89*	Mary Ames	3:23:06

(continued)

Masters Half-Marathon Records—*Continued*

Men's American Records

Age	Name	Time
40–44	Barry Brown	1:06:25
45–49	Oscar Moore	1:09:15
50–54	Norm Green	1:09:30
55–59	Norm Green	1:10:23
60–64	Gaylon Jorgensen	1:17:04
65–69	Michael Bertolini	1:23:50
70–74	Mac Osborn	1:34:22
75–79	Ed Benham	1:37:51
80–84	Ed Benham	1:40:30
85–89*	Max Popper	2:26:46

Women's World 1-Hour Records

Age	Name (Country)	Distance
40–44	Linda Sipprelle (U.S.)	9 mi. 1197 yd.
45–49	Marilyn Harbin (U.S.)	9 mi. 376 yd.
50–54	Nola Bruhn (U.S.)	8 mi. 1009 yd.
55–59	Barbara Meadows (U.S.)	8 mi. 638 yd.
60–64	Marcie Trent (U.S.)	8 mi. 219 yd.
65–69	Gerry Davidson (U.S.)	7 mi. 400 yd.
70–74	Alice Werbel (U.S.)	6 mi. 52 yd.
75–79	Marilla Salisbury (U.S.)	4 mi. 167 yd.
80–84	Mary Ames (U.S.)	4 mi. 668 yd.

Men's World 1-Hour Records

Age	Name (Country)	Distance
40–44	William Stoddard (Britain)	11 mi. 1309 yd.
45–49	Alain Mimoun (France)	11 mi. 1268 yd.
50–54	Alain Mimoun	11 mi. 954 yd.
55–59	John Gilmour (Australia)	10 mi. 1194 yd.
60–64	John Gilmour	10 mi. 831 yd.
65–69	John Gilmour	9 mi. 1540 yd.
70–74	John Gilmour	9 mi. 1083 yd.
75–79	Ed Benham (U.S.)	8 mi. 899 yd.
80–84	Paul Spangler (U.S.)	7 mi. 946 yd.
85–89	Paul Spangler	6 mi. 472 yd.
90–94	Herb Kirk (U.S.)	3 mi. 1368 yd.

16

Competing in the Classic

What It Takes to Make It through a Marathon

The marathon is home turf for Priscilla and Bill. They're best known for what they do there, though they now do it but once or twice a year.

The marathon, anyone's marathon, requires special effort and focus. You may wake up one morning and decide on a whim to enter a 10-K that day. But you wouldn't think of approaching a marathon that way.

We introduced marathon training in chapter 12, where the goal was to finish the race. Now, we're talking about *improving* in one.

For you, this may simply mean running faster than before. Or it may mean breaking a barrier—be it 3 or 4 hours, or fractions thereof. It may mean qualifying for the Boston Marathon, or maybe even setting an age-group record for the course.

The Long Climb

The marathon is the Mount Everest of running. It's a peak that every runner dreams of scaling at least once, and one that you may have already conquered. Doing it again—and doing it better—may be easier than you think. (Though it's never truly easy.)

You don't need to commit your whole life to marathon training. Making one change a week in your routine for one season of the year should carry you to a better marathon.

Granted, this one change is substantial. It requires you to greatly increase the length of that run or the amount of race-pace training. But you run normally —even slightly easier than usual—the rest of the time. (See "Marathon Plans" below.)

Whether you choose this program or another one, remember that *all* effective programs share three common elements: long runs, fast runs, and easy runs. Only the amounts of each differ from plan to plan.

You must train far enough to cope with the race distance, fast enough to handle its pace, and easily enough to recover between the long and fast work.

Marathon Plans

Our sample three-month training plan for the marathon concentrates on the critical days set aside for running either short, fast, or easy.

Long runs, taken every other week, are the key to your success. Start them about a half-hour longer than the time of your longest recent run. Gradually increase their length until they approach the projected *time* (not distance) of your marathon. Eliminate the early weeks if you're already running that long.

On weeks between long runs, shorter races and training runs maintain speed and excitement. Race if you wish, but only up to 10-K, so you'll recover in time for the next week's big effort. Or run your projected marathon pace for about half the length of the latest long run.

The other six days of each week are spent recovering and relaxing. Run no more than an hour on these days. Give yourself one day off a week, preferably right after the big day.

Week	Big Day
1	1½ hours, walking breaks optional
2	Short race, or 45 minutes steady
3	1½ to 2 hours, walks optional
4	Short race, or 45 to 60 minutes steady
5	1¾ to 2½ hours, walks optional
6	Short race, or 1 to 1¼ hours steady
7	2 to 3 hours, walks optional
8	Short race, or 1 to 1½ hours steady
9	2½ to 3½ hours, walks optional
10	Short race, or 1¼ to 1¾ hours
11	3 to 4 hours with walks
12	Nothing long or fast
13	Nothing long or fast
14	Marathon race

Training Longer

You're now the veteran of at least one marathon. You've had the good experience of finishing, and perhaps a bad experience or two while struggling to reach the finish line. But the experience has given you a new challenge: You now have a PR to better.

The groundwork for improvement begins with your long run. Even experienced marathoners seldom, if ever, run 26.2 miles in training. The distance far exceeds their daily averages, so the long run should become your critical focus.

Focus now on improving the effectiveness of your long run. Make refinements in the length, pace, and frequency of these runs based on your previous marathon training experience by answering the following questions.

1. Were my long runs long enough? They should still, in most cases, last as long as the predicted time of your marathon. (See "The Marathon Time Challenge" on page 140 for your projections.)

If you fell short of that time quota, you need to spend more time on the road.

If you met the quota and still felt inadequately prepared, switch from running by time to running by miles. You need to push your mileage closer to the marathon distance.

2. Were my long runs fast enough? You shouldn't attempt to run them at maximum marathon pace. But training pace should still bear some resemblance to that of the race.

If you took more than a week to recover from a long run, reduce your pace. The pace took too high a toll.

If your training runs felt too easy compared with the racing effort, then increase your training pace somewhat. And if you took walking breaks before, decrease their length and number.

3. Were my long runs frequent enough? You never need to run long more than once a week, but you should be taking long runs at least once every three weeks.

If you grew impatient last time with a schedule that called for a long run every two or three weeks, increase your long runs to every week or two—provided this gives you adequate recovery time. If, however, you tried a weekly long run and grew chronically weary, space it out by an extra week or even two.

Training Faster

Most runners in the marathon are running just to finish. So why should they be concerned with speed? There are good reasons:

1. It lifts you out of a one-pace rut.

2. It adds variety and enjoyment to your marathon training.

3. It gives you something challenging to do on the weekends between long runs.

The Marathon Time Challenge

Races requiring 2 or more hours to complete—from 25-K to the marathon—all require similar training and tactics.

This table lists comparable times for these long road races. It is based on the 5 percent formula explained in chapter 13. As the distance doubles, runners typically slow by 5 percent—or speed up by that amount at half the distance. (See "Predictable Pace" on page 111.)

Times here are rounded to the nearest full minute.

Refer to your most recent race time in the table to find your *predicted* time for your upcoming race. If you raced a 1:25 25-K, for example, you can predict a 2:30 marathon.

Marathon	25-K	30-K	20-Mile
2:15	1:17	1:33	1:41
2:20	1:20	1:37	1:44
2:25	1:22	1:40	1:48
2:30	1:25	1:43	1:52
2:35	1:28	1:47	1:56
2:40	1:31	1:50	1:59
2:45	1:34	1:54	2:03
2:50	1:37	1:57	2:07
2:55	1:39	2:01	2:11
3:00	1:42	2:04	2:14
3:05	1:45	2:08	2:18
3:10	1:48	2:11	2:22
3:15	1:51	2:14	2:26
3:20	1:54	2:18	2:29
3:25	1:56	2:21	2:33
3:30	1:59	2:25	2:37
3:35	2:02	2:28	2:40
3:40	2:05	2:32	2:44
3:45	2:08	2:35	2:48
3:50	2:11	2:39	2:52
3:55	2:14	2:42	2:55
4:00	2:16	2:46	2:59
4:05	2:19	2:49	3:03
4:10	2:22	2:52	3:07
4:15	2:25	2:56	3:10
4:20	2:28	2:59	3:14
4:25	2:31	3:03	3:18
4:30	2:33	3:06	3:21
4:35	2:36	3:10	3:25
4:40	2:39	3:13	3:29
4:45	2:42	3:17	3:33
4:50	2:45	3:20	3:36
4:55	2:48	3:23	3:40

The first goal of marathon training is to prepare for its distance. But it should also be a time to maintain your speed at such a long distance. It's easy to neglect your speedwork when you're piling up all those miles.

A few speed runs will benefit any marathoner and make you more efficient. Speedwork can translate to faster racing with no apparent increase in effort. And, an occasional speed run makes a marathon pace seem easy by comparison.

The best place to build speed is in short races. Plan to enter some 5-, 8-, and 10-K's on alternate weekends between long runs. Be sure to limit these distances to 10-K. That way, you'll get the full speed benefit and an easy recovery. Also, allow at least two weeks between your last short race and your marathon.

In lieu of a race, take a semilong run. Go about half the length of your last long session. If that was 3 hours, run 1½ hours steadily (without walking breaks), at your projected pace for the marathon—or slightly faster.

Long runs simulate the full marathon distance, but the necessary walk breaks slow your overall pace. Fast runs mimic full racing pace, but at a partial distance. Combine these two elements in the race.

Resting Up

The marathon is your graduation ceremony—a 26-mile, 385-yard victory lap. The hardest work, the buildup of distance and speed that went on for months, is behind you.

Don't try to pack in any extra work in the last week or two. You draw marathon energy from a reservoir of fitness you built gradually over the previous several months. Hard work in the final days does nothing but drain that pool at the worst possible time.

Go into the race well-rested. Allow two or three weeks between your last long run and the marathon. Run minimum amounts (about a half-hour) during the last week, and rest completely the final day or two. Save your trained-in strength for when it counts.

The Pace of Success

"The wall" that marathoners talk about shouldn't give you nightmares. Oh, it is a very real part of the event—but not an inevitable part. Those runners who hit it have made mistakes in training or in pacing.

Pace the marathon by treating it as two separate events—equal in size and as closely matched as possible in time, but very different in approach (see "Marathon Pacing" on page 143). As we discussed in chapter 13, run the first half as if it were a warmup. Hold back when your natural urge is to speed up. If people want to pass you, let them go.

Race the second half. Push on when your natural urge is to slow down. Take pleasure in passing the people who had passed you earlier.

Postmarathon Blues

There is life after the marathon, even though you may not think so in the immediate postrace days and weeks. Once you've thought through the race and talked it out, once the euphoria has worn off, the "postmarathon blues" are likely to follow.

We're not talking about postrace pains. You expect stiffness in the thighs and calves, and you wear your limp like a badge of courage.

What you may not be prepared to deal with is the subtle damage: the lingering weariness in your legs, yes, but an even more devastating weariness of spirit. You don't feel like running.

This effect is partly psychological. The goal that pulled you up the mountain for months is gone now, and nothing new has yet replaced it.

Some loss of enthusiasm is inevitable. The psyche will heal along with the body, however—if you give it enough time. This takes more time than most runners imagine, and the worst mistake you can make now is to rush that natural timetable.

Don't think that you are recovered from the marathon once the muscle soreness disappears a few days after the marathon. Don't beg for trouble by forcing yourself back into full training and racing before your energy debt has been repaid.

Too many marathoners hobble into doctors' offices a week or two after the race and complain, "I had no problems in the marathon, then this happened in yesterday's long run. What bad luck!"

Luck has nothing to do with it. Heaping abuse on an already overworked body yielded that predictable result.

Marathoning is as destructive as it is exciting. Don't miss the excitement, but take extreme care to clear away the damage. Recover from the marathon as if it were an injury, and give yourself a month or more to heal with easy running.

PW Priscilla on Her Training

I've often thought that the hardest part of a marathon is not the race itself but the training for it. You have to build up your fitness and think about the marathon for such a long time.

Yet, my training for the biggest race I've run to date, the 1984 Olympic Marathon in Los Angeles, was actually very relaxed. Dave set out a program, and I felt no urge to do a bit more just in case.

I remember thinking at the end, "Look, I carried out the schedule to a T." I was confident that I'd done all the training that was necessary.

In Los Angeles, no one expected me to do extremely well. Although I had no reputation, I wasn't going to L.A. just to occupy a seat on the plane or for the chance to take part. I really was focusing in on the bronze medal, which of course I missed, but I still finished sixth.

Marathon Pacing

While an evenly paced marathon is the ideal, splits for each half of the race can vary by as much as 5 seconds per mile — 2:11 total — without hurting your result. As the spread grows wider, your final time suffers.

The table below lists the fastest and slowest recommended halfway splits at various marathon speeds. Find your predicted final time (see "The Marathon Time Challenge" on page 140), then plan to run each half of the race within the range of maximum splits listed.

After the race, analyze your time by subtracting the faster half from the slower. If they differ by more than 2:11, adjust your starting pace the next time you run this distance.

Maximum splits for other long road races are 1:08 for 25-K, 1:33 for 30-K, and 1:40 for 20 miles.

Marathon	Even Half-Marathons	Maximum Splits
2:15	1:07:30	1:06:25–1:08:36
2:20	1:10:00	1:08:55–1:11:06
2:25	1:12:30	1:11:25–1:13:36
2:30	1:15:00	1:13:55–1:16:06
2:35	1:17:30	1:16:25–1:18:36
2:40	1:20:00	1:18:55–1:21:06
2:45	1:22:30	1:21:25–1:23:36
2:50	1:25:00	1:23:55–1:26:06
2:55	1:27:30	1:26:25–1:28:36
3:00	1:30:00	1:28:55–1:31:06
3:05	1:32:30	1:31:25–1:33:36
3:10	1:35:00	1:33:55–1:36:06
3:15	1:37:30	1:36:25–1:38:36
3:20	1:40:00	1:38:55–1:41:06
3:25	1:42:30	1:41:25–1:43:36
3:30	1:45:00	1:43:55–1:46:06
3:35	1:47:30	1:46:25–1:48:36
3:40	1:50:00	1:48:55–1:51:06
3:45	1:52:30	1:51:25–1:53:36
3:50	1:55:00	1:53:55–1:56:06
3:55	1:57:30	1:56:25–1:58:36
4:00	2:00:00	1:58:55–2:01:06
4:05	2:02:30	2:01:25–2:03:36
4:10	2:05:00	2:03:55–2:06:06
4:15	2:07:30	2:06:25–2:08:36
4:20	2:10:00	2:08:55–2:11:06
4:25	2:12:30	2:11:25–2:13:36
4:30	2:15:00	2:13:55–2:16:06
4:35	2:17:30	2:16:25–2:18:36
4:40	2:20:00	2:18:55–2:21:06
4:45	2:22:30	2:21:25–2:23:36
4:50	2:25:00	2:23:55–2:26:06
4:55	2:27:30	2:26:25–2:28:36

In 1987, it was a different ball game because we'd been in the sport a bit longer and I'd put up some good performances. I was more focused. No more of that "Let's just see what we can do."

For the London Marathon in 1987, I'd done the basework in New Zealand and had run 2:38 in Nagoya, Japan, off that training. That was just to educate the body about the distance. We've come to believe that you can do a marathon like a kick-start for a real one two months later.

The Nagoya Marathon was really just a confirmation race that my aerobic training had been done properly, that I could finish the distance and still feel fresh. Then, ten weeks later, after much sharpening, I ran my 2:26:51 in London, an hour faster than my first marathon.

My marathon training comes in three phases. Dave puts down on paper

Masters Marathon Records

Priscilla Welch's and John Campbell's equally incredible times of 2:26:51 and 2:11:04 lead the list of world age-group bests, according to *Runner's World* magazine. The Athlete's Congress Statistics (TACSTATS) provides the American records, as of early 1991. (An * indicates the fastest pending road time in age-groups with no ratified record.)

Men's World Records

Age	Name (Country)	Time
40–44	John Campbell (New Zealand)	2:11:04
45–49	Jack Foster (New Zealand)	2:17:29
50–54	Jack Foster	2:20:28
55–59	Erik Ostbye (Sweden)	2:26:35
60–64	Derek Turnbull (New Zealand)	2:38:47
65–69	Clive Davies (U.S.)	2:42:49
70–74	Monty Montgomery (U.S.)	3:07:26

Women's World Records

Age	Name (Country)	Time
40–44	Priscilla Welch (Britain)	2:26:51
45–49	Evy Palm (Sweden)	2:31:05
50–54	Denise Alfvoet (Belgium)	2:51:46
55–59	Margaret Miller (U.S.)	3:07:21
60–64	Helen Dick (U.S.)	3:15:30

what he'd like me to do for each phase.

I roughly follow that plan. But if I'm not comfortable, I needn't force myself through a workout just because the schedule calls for it. Some days, I can't carry out the plan exactly.

There are times in training for a marathon when I get tired, tense, and grouchy. Dave understands, because he goes through the same while training for his triathlons. We're both evil when we're tired.

I just have to take plenty of rest when doing a lot of training. Even though there's always something else in the house to do, I've got to find the time to pick up a book and put my feet up. During serious marathon training, I've got to say, "Whoa, it's time for a nap."

It's exciting to move from the first phase of training to the second, because I

Men's American Records

Age	Name	Time
40–44	William Hall	2:23:08
45–49	John Brennand	2:28:46
50–54	Norm Green	2:29:11
55–59	Alex Ratelle	2:37:40
60–64	Clive Davies	2:42:44
65–69	Clive Davies	2:42:49
70–74	Monty Montgomery	3:07:26
75–79	Ed Benham	3:34:42
80–84	Paul Spangler	4:53:11
85–89*	Paul Spangler	5:21:51

Women's American Records

Age	Name	Time
40–44	Laurie Binder	2:42:29
45–49	Sandra Kiddy	2:53:22
50–54	Marion Irvine	2:52:02
55–59	Margaret Miller	3:07:21
60–64	Helen Dick	3:15:30
65–69	Helen Dick	3:48:10
70–74	Mavis Lindgren	4:37:37
75–79	Mavis Lindgren	4:56:30
80–84	Ida Mintz	5:10:04

think, "Oh, the race is getting nearer!" Then going into the third phase, it's, "Not far to go now!"

I just love the last three weeks before a marathon, when you're really face to face with the race and you're peaking and feeling fresh. I look forward to that feeling, although I don't really care for the last three days before the marathon.

It's not at all easy to sleep the night before a marathon. Dave has always told me that if you can get a good sleep the night *before* the night before, then that's sufficient.

We've often stayed in hotels that are noisy, where couples are partying or fighting next door. Before the 1985 Pittsburgh Marathon, we changed rooms twice.

I try not to let this bother me. If it does, it will upset my performance. Because of the travel involved in competing, I'm used to running on little sleep anyway. ■

BR Bill on His Training

My best results always have come from running high mileage before marathons, getting really strong. I don't do this with extremely long runs like 25 or 30 miles, but through total mileage—nonstop high mileage adding up to 120 or more miles a week.

So I concentrate on doing double workouts. Even on my long day of the weekend, if I ran 18 to 21 miles in the morning, I'd go out in the afternoon or evening, too. I put in a lot of miles that way.

Though my training was more aerobic-based than anaerobic-based, I always did some speedwork—everything from repeat quarter-miles up to repeat 2-miles. One of my best workouts was four to six times a mile at about 10-K race pace. The main reason I did so poorly in the 1976 Olympics (40th place) was that I avoided speedwork because of an injured foot.

I've been known to overrace. There were times in my career when I ran for more than the recommended two marathons a year.

If I had stuck to two in 1978, when I won both Boston and New York City, I probably would have been ranked number one in the world instead of second. But six weeks after New York, I went to Fukuoka, Japan, and placed fifth there. It was at the end of a complete year of pushing.

My most satisfying marathon came at Boston the next spring. I set my PR of 2:09:28 and beat Toshihiko Seko of Japan, who had won at Fukuoka and ranked first in the world for 1978. I aimed more for that one race than any other, including the Olympics.

My biggest mistake in the marathon has probably been not understanding how much recovery you need, not knowing how different marathon training is from 10-K training. You don't want to do too little or too much in your training. Maybe instead of doing the usual schedule of alternating hard and easy days, you should run hard one day and easy the next two days or more.

Older runners underestimate the component of rest in their training. When you were younger, you could recover much faster than you can as a master. Now you have to be a little more careful in your training. ■

17

Mastering the Mile

Improving Your Speed on the Track

Bill Rodgers typifies the long-time runner. He started running track in high school and kept at it through college.

Though reborn as a road racer in the early 1970s, Bill continued his track racing throughout that decade. He nearly made the Olympic 10,000-meter team in 1976, sampled the European track circuit in 1978, and set his world 25-K track record in 1979.

Priscilla Welch, though, is more typical of today's runners. She started late and without ever dreaming of track glory as young Bill Rodgers did. She became a road specialist who seldom raced on the track. Yet she now trains there more than Bill does.

Track training and racing—centered on the mile—have much to offer, even to a road runner.

Magic of the Mile

Track has gone metric, with one major exception. Only the mile carries over from an archaic system of measurement as an official world-record distance.

Yet this relic remains the sport's most glamorous event and the single most important time by which runners are judged. "So you're a runner," someone will say at a party. "What's your best mile?" Quoting a 1500-meter time won't do.

We race by meters on the track and kilometers on the road, but we take our splits and weigh our pace by minutes per *mile*. The mile still is the central distance in American running.

The 4-minute mile is a standard of excellence known by even the most casual of sports fans. Now, masters men are closing in on that barrier (with Wilson Waigwa of Kenya coming closest so far at 4:05.39).

Whether you're running a mile for the first time or returning to it after a long time away, it reveals many truths about racing on the track. Some come as pleasant surprises, some as rude shocks.

The track is at once the best and worst place to race. To appreciate the best of it, we first need to recognize the worst.

Juha Vaatainen, a Finn who once was the world's best track runner, said in his heyday, "I don't like to go around a track. Stadiums were invented for spectators, not runners. We have nature, and that's much better."

Road racers feel confined on a track that measures only 400 meters or 440 yards to the lap. They see the same scenery four times in the space of a mile and quickly grow bored with running in circles.

When a track race goes poorly, there is no place to hide. This isn't a road run, where you make brief appearances at the start and finish and disappear for a half-hour or more in between. Spectators at the track can watch every runner's every step, and runners can see exactly how far the leaders are ahead.

On the other hand, there are bonuses to track racing, too. When you're racing well, there's no better place to display your talents, since you're never out of sight.

Track racing also features a mathematical perfection and a simplicity that road and cross-country runs lack. Since one track is pretty much like any other, the times carry greater comparative value. And because all tracks are level and only require making left turns, you don't worry about reading the course but simply about running fast.

Other truisms from the track:

• The mile is good speed training. A simple way to gain (or regain or maintain) the speed that translates into faster times at all the longer distances is to follow the one-one-one plan: 1 mile, at least 1 minute faster than easy training pace, one day a week.

• A track race is a great place do this speed training. Running the mile 1 minute (or more) faster than normal seems less difficult and more appetizing in the company of other runners than it would be by yourself.

• The racing gets better with repetition. The less speedwork you have done in the past, the more dramatically you can improve your mile time in a series of races. With each one, you shift more smoothly into a higher gear.

Bill on Track

I ran the mile and 2-mile in high school and college, but with little success. Even then, my interests and training pointed me to the longer distances.

I might have competed well in the 10,000-meter or 6-mile during college. I certainly was doing enough mileage to prepare for it. But there weren't many chances to race at this distance in the late 1960s.

As it was, I won most of my shorter races at a small school, Wesleyan University, in a conference of small schools. My sights were set on winning on that level, and I didn't look beyond it.

After my postcollege "retirement," I returned to running as a marathoner. But I also dabbled in track racing for many years.

Mile Plans

Everyone asks, "What is your best mile time?" because everyone sort of knows what times mean at this classic track distance. If you aren't proud of your answer, you *can* improve your PR.

Your past attempts may have felt like an all-out sprint because you weren't accustomed to racing at such a fast pace. But you can adjust to it by running faster, more often.

Adopt two short but fast sessions and a race each week for about a month to reach your peak. Include in your speedwork a tempo run and intervals at mile race pace, and 800-meter races at well below mile pace. (See chapters 11 and 12 for detailed advice on fast training.)

Start each speed session with a thorough warmup and end it with an easy cooldown run. Limit your distance runs to an easy hour or less on some of the days between speedwork.

The following sample weekly plan is aimed at a mile, but it can be modified for any track race, 1500 to 5000 meters, by changing the length of the fast runs.

Day	Plan
1	Optional day: easy run, cross-training, or rest
2	Tempo run: 800 meters at mile race pace
3	Optional day: easy run, cross-training, or rest
4	Intervals: four 200s at mile race pace
5	Optional day: easy run, cross-training, or rest
6	Mile race at top speed, *or* 800-meter race at close to top speed
7	Optional day: easy run, cross-training, or rest

In fact, one of the most satisfying races of my life came at the 1976 Olympic Trials. I ran the time needed to qualify for the 10,000 trial with a 28:42 at the Penn Relays in late April, made the Olympic Marathon team at Eugene, Oregon, in mid-May, and then returned to track Trials in June.

I was very excited to be running in a high-level track meet. There were TV cameras and the whole works.

We reached the halfway point in 13:55, which gave me a PR for 5000 meters. Frank Shorter got away from me, then Craig Virgin.

Garry Bjorklund had lost a shoe early in the race. But with 300 meters to go, running with one bare foot, he passed me to sew up the third spot on the team. Though I finished fourth, I was thrilled to drop my PR to 28:04.4.

As it turned out, I could have run the 10,000 in Montreal. Frank Shorter passed up that event, and I was next in line for his spot. But my coach, Billy Squires, and I had already decided that even if I made the 10-K team, I would run only the marathon.

Only one other year did I attempt a series of high-quality track races. That was the summer of 1978 in Europe.

I was still running very high mileage then and doing some heavy-duty road racing. I'd won the Boston Marathon that April, and would come back from Europe to win the Falmouth Road Race in August.

My first track race in Europe was terrible. I had trained about 150 miles a week right up to that 10,000 in London and hadn't prepared well for competing on the track.

I thought I was going to beat Brendan Foster of Britain, but I didn't realize how important it was to do anaerobic work. Foster was probably doing 50 miles of high-quality training a week.

Foster broke the European record with 27:30 in that race and lapped me. I finished eighth in 29:12.

Better rested for my next race, another 10,000 in Stockholm a week later, I just missed my PR with 28:04.8. Toshihiko Seko of Japan, a marathoner like me, won in 27:51.

My final race in Europe was a 5000 in Oslo. I bettered my PR with 13:42 and had a chance to win with a half-lap to go, then four runners left me in their dust with their finishing kicks.

Racing on the track was both exciting and intimidating to me. It was exciting because it was so different from road racing, where times can vary so much and where tactics play less of a role. In track, there's a lot more precision involved.

Yet it was intimidating because you need so much talent to race on the track. If you don't have a kick, you're built to lose. You're going to get dusted, because even the longer track races usually come down to who has the most speed at the finish.

That summer in Europe taught me that I wasn't fast enough to be a winner on the track. It gave me great appreciation for the achievers in track and the work they put in.

The Mile Time Challenge

A family of races surrounds the mile. Distances from 1500 to 5000 meters all require similar training and tactics.

This table lists comparable times for these track races. It is based on the 5 percent formula: As the distance doubles, runners typically slow by 5 percent — or speed up by that amount at half the distance. (See "Predictable Pace" on page 111.)

Refer to your most recent race time in the table to find your *predicted* time for your upcoming race. If you raced a 6:40 mile, for example, you can predict that you will run a 6:10 1500.

Mile	1500	3000	5000
4:00	3:42	7:55	13:45
4:10	3:51	8:15	14:20
4:20	4:01	8:35	14:54
4:30	4:10	8:55	15:29
4:40	4:19	9:14	16:04
4:50	4:29	9:34	16:36
5:00	4:38	9:54	17:12
5:10	4:47	10:14	17:46
5:20	4:56	10:34	18:20
5:30	5:06	10:53	18:55
5:40	5:15	11:13	19:30
5:50	5:24	11:33	20:04
6:00	5:33	11:53	20:39
6:10	5:43	12:13	21:12
6:20	5:52	12:32	21:47
6:30	6:01	12:52	22:22
6:40	6:10	13:12	22:56
6:50	6:18	13:32	23:30
7:00	6:29	13:52	24:05
7:10	6:38	14:11	24:40
7:20	6:47	14:31	25:14
7:30	6:57	14:51	25:48
7:40	7:06	15:11	26:23
7:50	7:15	15:31	26:57

That tour also made me appreciate road racing even more than before. I felt out of place with our touring group. I didn't know anybody, even the Americans, and didn't have much in common with the sprinters and jumpers. By contrast, I feel at home among road runners wherever we meet on the racing circuit. ■

 Priscilla on Track

I'm no stranger to the track. While I haven't raced there very much, track training is critical to my preparation for marathons.

I have a love/hate relationship with track workouts. I like what they do for me but don't always like doing them. Track sessions can be slogs, yet they've got to be done.

I use the track for pacework purely because it gives me exact distances and times. Pace is easier to gauge here than on the road because I can monitor each quarter-mile.

I'm only on the track about once every two weeks in the conditioning phase of training. Then in the last six to eight weeks before a major race, I train on the track twice a week. Typical workouts are an interval session like eight 1000s or a 3000- to 5000-meter time trial.

Despite this familiarity with the oval, I've never had a track racing career. My only real success there came in 1984, shortly before I became a master.

At age 39, I ran two 10,000-meter races in England and won them both by a lap. This was a bittersweet experience.

These races were part of a three-race series that offered prize money of 1000£ to the winner, and one of the races was for the British championship. I missed one of the three because I was at the Olympics, and as a result didn't win the series prize. And even though I won the championship race, I wasn't awarded the title because the official said I'd filled in the entry form incorrectly.

As a master, I'm credited with only one world track best—the single-age 5000 mark of 16:13.8 for 41-year-olds. That record is something of a joke, because I've *averaged* faster times than that for both halves of a road 10-K.

Also, my 5000 time is slower than Evy Palm's over-40 record of 16:02.88, set when she was 43. Evy is the greatest master track woman to date. Her times are phenomenal. At age 44, she ran the 10,000 in 33:00.78—which was more than a minute faster than the masters record. Then she got better with age: 32:42.25 at 44, 32:41.98 at 45, and 32:34.05 at 46.

Great as Evy Palm is, though, I think I'm capable of running at her level or better. After all, I've beaten her in both of the marathons that we ran together —the 1984 Olympics and 1985 New York City—and my road time of 32:14 is faster than hers from the track.

I fancy doing some track racing. It fits nicely into my plans this year. I plan to do only one marathon and then not do another until 1992, when I attempt to make the Olympic team for Barcelona. ■

Mile Pacing

You seek an evenly paced mile, but the two halves of the race don't need to be perfectly matched. Their pace can vary by 5 seconds without hurting your final time.

The table below lists the fastest and slowest recommended halfway splits at various mile speeds. Plan to run each half of your predicted time within the maximum splits listed.

After the race, analyze your time by subtracting the faster half from the slower. If they differ by more than 5 seconds, plan to adjust your starting pace the next time you run this distance.

Maximum splits for other short road races are 4 seconds for 1500 meters, 9 seconds for 3000, and 10 seconds for 5000.

Mile	Even Half-Miles	Maximum Splits
4:00	2:00	1:58–2:03
4:10	2:05	2:03–2:08
4:20	2:10	2:08–2:13
4:30	2:15	2:13–2:18
4:40	2:20	2:18–2:23
4:50	2:25	2:23–2:28
5:00	2:30	2:28–2:33
5:10	2:35	2:33–2:38
5:20	2:40	2:38–2:43
5:30	2:45	2:43–2:48
5:40	2:50	2:48–2:53
5:50	2:55	2:53–2:58
6:00	3:00	2:58–3:03
6:10	3:05	3:03–3:08
6:20	3:10	3:08–3:13
6:30	3:15	3:13–3:18
6:40	3:20	3:18–3:23
6:50	3:25	3:23–3:28
7:00	3:30	3:28–3:33
7:10	3:35	3:33–3:38
7:20	3:40	3:38–3:43
7:30	3:45	3:43–3:48
7:40	3:50	3:48–3:53
7:50	3:55	3:53–3:58

Masters Mile Records

Women masters long since have broken the 5-minute mile barrier. Men have gone under 4:10 and are zeroing in on 4 minutes.

The annual booklet *Masters Age Records* keeps track of progress in this and all other events. (For more information, write to *National Masters News,* Box 16597, North Hollywood, CA 91615.) Shirley Dietderich compiles the women's records, and Peter Mundle the men's. Here, they list the best mile times through early 1991.

Men's World Records

Age	Name (Country)	Time
40–44	Wilson Waigwa (Kenya)	4:05.39
45–49	Dave Sirl (New Zealand)	4:16.75
50–54	Tom Roberts (Australia)	4:30.06
55–59	Jack Ryan (Australia)	4:40.4
60–64	Rune Bergman (Sweden)	5:04.36
65–69	Jack Ryan	5:05.61
70–74	Scotty Carter (U.S.)	5:32.4
75–79	Harold Chapson (U.S.)	6:15.1
80–84	Harold Chapson	6:43.3
85–89	Josef Galia (West Germany)	8:04.7
90–94	Herb Kirk (U.S.)	13:43.6

Women's World and American Records

Age	Name (Country)	Time
40–44	Doris Heritage (U.S.)	4:54.89
45–49	Sandra Knott (U.S.)	5:14.7
50–54	Jeanne Hoagland (U.S.)	5:29.39
55–59	Margaret Miller (U.S.)	5:50.6
60–64	Pat Dixon (U.S.)	6:35.0
65–69	Rosamund Dashwood (Canada)	6:41.64
	Pat Dixon	6:55.6
70–74	Pat Dixon	7:26.0
75–79	Ivy Granstrom (Canada)	8:58.8
80–84	Marilla Salisbury (U.S.)	12:57.0

(continued)

Masters Mile Records—*Continued*

Men's American Records

Age	Name	Time
40–44	Larry Almberg	4:06.70
45–49	Mike Manley	4:28.02
50–54	Bill Fitzgerald	4:32.2
55–59	Don Gammie	4:46.5
60–64	David Stevenson	5:14.2
65–69	Monty Montgomery	5:22.0
70–74	Scotty Carter	5:32.4
75–79	Harold Chapson	6:15.1
80–84	Harold Chapson	6:43.3
85–89	Herb Kirk	12:23.6
90–94	Herb Kirk	12:43.6

18

Off the Beaten Path

The Joy of Training
and Racing Cross-Country

Priscilla Welch grew up in a cross-country country. "Harrier" running has long been a staple of the British club system, where the season stretches from fall through early spring. The Brits favor true cross-country—not manicured golf courses, but muddy fields with fences to jump and streams to ford. But because Priscilla started running late and abroad, she wasn't schooled in cross-country, British style.

In Britain and the Commonwealth countries such as Australia and New Zealand, running is a club sport. Athletes can join at any age and remain members for as long as they wish. The membership leans heavily toward distance runners, and the running is centered on cross-country.

In the United States, by contrast, cross-country is largely a school sport. Races are shorter (and courses easier) than in Britain, and so are the racing season (lasting only about two months in the fall) and the cross-country careers (which seldom extend past high school or college graduation).

Bill Rodgers's running career began with American-style cross-country. He succeeded in his first international cross-country competition despite the limitations of his early running. He hardly ran any cross-country between his last college season, in 1969, and the winter of 1975. His experience in the international style of running consisted of a single race—the trials for selecting the U.S. national team, where he ran the cross-country race of his life.

At the 1975 World Cross-Country Championships in Morocco, Bill won a bronze medal against runners far more experienced than himself. He used this breakthrough into world-class running as a springboard for his first Boston Marathon victory a month later.

The Maker of Champions

The toughness and tactical savvy gained from cross-country serve runners well in any arena. Norway's Grete Waitz, who broke the world marathon record four times, was a five-time World Cross-Country champion. Portugal's Carlos Lopes, Olympic Marathon gold medalist and world record-setter, won his third World Cross-Country title at age 38.

Five-time World Cross-Country champion Doris Brown Heritage of the United States holds the world masters mile record. World Cross-Country winner Joyce Smith from Britain set the masters marathon record that Priscilla would break.

Britain exported its harrier tradition to New Zealand. John Campbell, Jack Foster, and Derek Turnbull — all products of that system — are the world's fastest marathoners for the forties, fifties, and sixties age-groups, respectively. Australia shares a similar heritage, and it has produced the world's fastest over-70 runner, John Gilmour. Gilmour, Turnbull, and New Zealander Roger Robinson, 50, all won World Cross-Country championships for their divisions in 1989.

Britain exported Ray Hatton and Clive Davies to the United States. Drawing on cross-country background, they became two of the finest masters runners in U.S. history. Hatton still holds national over-50 track and road records in the 10-K and still is this country's fastest over-60 marathoner.

The World Veterans Championships feature a cross-country race equal in size and stature to events on the road and track. Here (as in the Worlds for younger runners) the cross-country courses are international in flavor. They include jumping barriers, a foreign experience to most American athletes. The World Vets races (unlike the youth Worlds, where women run only half as far as men) are the same 10-K distance for both sexes.

Cross-country isn't just a kids' sport around the world. So great are its beauties and benefits that it needs to grow up in the United States as well.

It can grow in several directions. Cross-country can mean off-road, off-track training. It can mean short but mountainous races such as the Dipsea in northern California, trail marathons such as the one on Catalina Island, or ultradistance trail runs-with-walks such as the Western States 100-mile.

In this chapter, we mainly examine standard 5-K to 15-K cross-country races. Even these events are anything but standardized in format.

It isn't too late for American masters to learn how to excel in these races. Consider the case of Marion Irvine, a Catholic nun who didn't begin running until she was 48 years old. She ran a 2:51 marathon and qualified for the U.S. Olympic Trials at age 54. Five years later, Sister Marion mastered the barriers well enough in her first attempt to win a World Veterans title in cross-country. She collected three more gold medals on the track and one on the road at the same meet.

Down-to-Earth Running

For runners like Bill Rodgers who started cross-country in their youth, it's their first love. But like most first romances, it has a hard time lasting past adolescence. Opportunities to race cross-country all but dry up during the late teens and early twenties, but memories don't fade.

On the mind's videotape, cross-country is crisp autumn days, damp grass, crunchy leaves. Time has edited out the heat of September, the snow of November, the fallen leaves that hide ankle-wrenching roots, the mud or snow that pulls off shoes, the hills so steep that you can reach out and touch them.

Long-time runner Fred Lawrence writes, "I sometimes think I like the *idea* of cross-country more than the fact of it. I'm also well aware of the negative side. But I don't want to give up the sport."

Lawrence speaks of cross-country as a separate sport, which it almost is because of its distinctions from road and track. He pleads with all runners who love cross-country to "encourage the big wheels of the sport to put more time and money into this aspect of distance running. Talk to them about how wonderful it would be to get a grass roots cross-country program going."

This takes some selling, not only with officials but also among runners. Late starters who were born and grew up on the roads may not trust surfaces that aren't smooth and hard.

The brave few novices who try cross-country feel awkward and confused on this unfamiliar ground (in part because today's shoes are made for road work, and their bulk discourages running anywhere else). Miles aren't marked, and splits may or may not be called. The distance might be shorter or longer than advertised.

But this is how cross-country should be. Concerns with exact times and distances are best left on the roads and tracks.

Runners accustomed to the preciseness of those other settings may not fall in love with cross-country at first. It's an acquired taste that grows slowly, but anyone who takes the time to acquire it never loses it.

Changing Seasons and Reasons

Cross-country season provides an interlude. It gives an escape from the roads and tracks, a break from concerns with splits and PRs, and a chance to put your feet back on real earth.

Track runners must spend most of their year racing on small ovals designed for spectators and coated with plastic for speed. Road runners leave the confining track but use even harder surfaces on courses designed for and shared by cars.

Track and road distances are standardized to allow anyone, anywhere, anytime to compare results, so track and road racers become very time-conscious.

Cross-country provides a vacation from racing against the clock. True cross-country uses only natural surfaces—dirt, grass or sand—and "natural" almost surely means rough and hilly rather than smooth and flat.

The rougher the course, the harder the work of measuring it and running it. The more natural the course is, the more the weather affects it—and the less your times mean.

If you hear that a track race is 10,000 meters long or that a road 10-K is "flat and fast," you know practically everything about it. There is no such thing as a standard cross-country course.

The distance of a 10-K could range from 5.8 to 6.3 miles. The course could run through a city park in New York, around a golf course in Kentucky, across a cornfield in Iowa, along a Rocky Mountain trail in Colorado, through a desert in New Mexico, or onto a beach in California.

Cross-country is as varied as the places it is run. For a change, we must face surfaces and terrains on their own natural terms instead of running in places modified for our ease and speed. Cross-country at its best is not a race against the clock but against the elements.

Changing Places and Paces

Training for a 10-K cross-country race doesn't look any different on paper (see "Cross-Country Plans" on the opposite page) than training for 10-K on the road or track. But the cross-country work *feels* different. Hills and soft, uneven ground make this training as unlike track or road practice as a mountain hike is to a city stroll.

You prepare for the hills and rough footing just as you make any big change: by adapting your training to it. Train much of the time this season on natural surfaces and terrain. Wear lighter, flimsier shoes that give a better "feel" for the ground and improve your sense of balance.

If possible, run the race course in training. At the very least, train on a surface and terrain similar to what you'll encounter in the race. Nowhere in running are these rehearsals more important, because cross-country courses can spring more surprises on you than any other.

Hills in the natural state tend to be steeper than those on roads, where the grade has been eased for the sake of auto traffic. Take this attitude about cross-country hills: Keep the *effort* constant, but let the pace shift with the grade. For instance, keep running at a 7-minute effort up a steep hill but shift down to a 9-minute pace. Then going downhill, shift up to a 6-minute pace but maintain the 7-minute effort.

Cross-Country Plans

In substance, cross-country training matches the preparation for a road or track race of similar distance. All of these programs combine the same elements—long runs, fast runs, and easy runs—in the same proportions.

Cross-country work differs from road or track in its setting. You can effectively speed train for road races on the track and for track races on the road, but you can only hone your cross-country skills by training over similar ground.

Racing on hilly terrain and on soft, uneven surfaces is a technique that cannot be learned by practicing on road terrain. Schedule at least your interval sessions and tempo runs on courses matching those of your races.

A sample program follows. It prepares you for a 10-K cross-country race, the distance that both men and women run at the World Veterans Championships. (Adjust the length of these suggested runs for races of other distances.) Consider working up to a 10-K peak in three weeks by scheduling a 5-K tempo run the first weekend, a 5-K race the second, and then the 10-K finale.

Day	Plan
1	Optional day: easy run, cross-training, or rest
2	Long run: 1 hour at much slower than race pace
3	Optional day: easy run, cross-training, or rest
4	Intervals: 3 times 1 mile at about 10-K race pace, *or* optional day the week of the big 10-K race
5	Optional day: easy run, cross-training, or rest
6	Big day: 5-K tempo run at about 10-K race pace, *or* 5-K cross-country race at close to top speed, *or* 10-K cross-country race at top speed
7	Optional day: easy run, cross-training, or rest

Changes in surface and terrain dictate a more flexible pace than you'd run on the track or roads. Plan on doing more surging and slowing than you would elsewhere, and worry less about meeting a timetable.

PW Priscilla on Cross-Country

Cross-country running was practically invented in England, so I rather shamefully admit that I've never run it properly. My experience is limited to a little racing, nothing spectacular, when we lived in Norway and the Shetland Islands.

My two Olympic Marathon teammates from 1984 are more typically British. Joyce Smith won the World Cross-Country title in 1972, the same year she competed in the first Olympic 1500-meter race for women. Later, like many other cross-country champions, she became one of the world's top marathoners.

Smith and I teamed up with Sarah Rowell at the Los Angeles Olympics. Because of injury problems, Rowell can't run much on roads anymore. But she's like a jackrabbit in cross-country and mountain running. She once beat all the women *and* men in an off-road marathon race.

Cross-country now clashes with my goal of training up for marathons, which are my bread and butter. But even a marathoner can profit by mixing trail running with road work.

Concrete and tarmac really batter your legs, and you need to give them a rest sometimes with easy runs on a trail. This also gives you a break from traffic and noise, and lets you relax.

My problem with trails is that my eyesight and running form aren't suited to this type of running. When I run on a trail that is partly shaded by trees, my eyes have trouble adjusting to the changes from bright sunlight to deep shade. This condition goes with being 46 years of age.

I've also got an economical way of running, which is to say that I don't lift my feet very high off the ground. If I'm running on a rocky trail and can't see well, I'm apt to take a nosedive.

I've fallen a couple of times, and on one occasion I actually broke a bone in my right hand. I stay clear of the lovely, woodsy trails in the Boulder area because they can also be hazardous to my road racing livelihood.

Having said this, please don't think I'm opposed to cross-country training and racing. I would still like to have a go at it a bit further down the line, if only because my career as a British runner would be woefully incomplete without this experience. ■

BR Bill on Cross-Country

My first organized sport was cross-country, which I liked right away after joining the high school team my sophomore year. I still love cross-country running and would train in the woods every day if it were possible. I envy the Europeans who can do much of their training on forest trails.

At Wesleyan University, Amby Burfoot and I did a lot of our running off the road—through brambles and briars, up and down hills on our hands and knees. Burfoot twice placed sixth in the NCAA Cross-Country Championships. He was one of the few runners I knew who set super-high goals, and I didn't even dream of being that successful.

I never even qualified for the NCAAs during college. The biggest meets I ever ran were regional championships.

After returning to the sport as primarily a road racer, I heard about the 1975 U.S. Cross-Country Trials in Gainesville, Florida. I decided to shoot for a spot on the team that would travel to the World Championships in Rabat, Morocco.

In the Trials, I raced Frank Shorter for the first time. He already was the Olympic Marathon champion, and I was in awe of him. He ran away from everyone else, but I still made the team.

I had done really high mileage that winter while getting ready for the Boston Marathon. I trained with the Greater Boston Track Club, and we often ran the hills on the marathon course. We were a competitive bunch, and we pushed each other hard.

I developed a lot of strength and in cross-country strength is hard to beat. My speed also was better than it had ever been. I ran lots of indoor 2-mile races, and in training I really forced the pace on my lunchtime 7-mile runs.

I arrived in Morocco very fit. The field was loaded with the best runners in the world from all events—milers, marathoners, steeplechasers, and 10-K stars. I didn't know who everyone was, which may have worked to my advantage, because running with them didn't psych me out.

It turned into a three-man race between Mariano Haro from Spain, Ian Stewart from Scotland, and me. They were both Olympic track finalists, and I was an international nobody. But I kept forcing the pace, hoping to break them.

With a half-mile to go, Stewart started kicking like hell. Then Haro passed me, too, and overtook the Scot to win. I finished third.

Having no idea I would do so well, I was in a state of shock after the race. During the medal ceremony, Haro and Stewart both waved to the crowd. Someone had to come up and lift my arm so I would wave, too.

This was a great day, probably the greatest ever in World Cross-Country, for the Americans. Our men's team finished fourth. Julie Brown, the individual winner, led the U.S. women to the team title. Bob Thomas and the junior men's team also won.

This also turned out to be the only great cross-country race of my life. A few weeks after returning from Morocco, I won the Boston Marathon. My road racing schedule soon became overwhelming, and I never again could focus on cross-country.

I still look forward to coming full circle someday, returning to the type of race that was my first love. ∎

19

A New Age of Champions

How Masters Running Will Expand and Improve

Bill and Priscilla are enjoying their time at the top of masters running. But they know that sooner or later they'll play lesser roles.

This is how over-40 racing works. This year's stars will be one birthday older by next year, and perhaps a step or two slower. By then new, theoretically faster masters will have entered this age-group. Even if the old guard maintains its speed, the new crop might inherently be more talented.

Each year brings greater talent into the masters ranks. Rod Dixon of New Zealand, an Olympic 1500-meter medalist and New York City Marathon winner, turned 40 in 1990 and became a threat to break any and all masters records.

Another New Zealander, Olympic 1500 champion and former mile record-holder John Walker, still competed in world-class open events in his late thirties. He will reach 40 in 1992. So will Eamonn Coghlan of Ireland, who holds the indoor mile record and won a world 5000 title.

Grete Waitz of Norway, many times a world record-setter in the marathon, will celebrate her 40th birthday in 1993. Francie Larrieu, member of four U.S. Olympic teams, will try for her fifth in 1992—shortly before turning 40.

This influx of talent disturbs neither Priscilla nor Bill. Without acknowledging any arbitrary time limit on her prime years, Priscilla recognizes that improvement isn't limitless. She has long called the highly competitive phase of her life "a pleasant interlude" between what came before her first PR and whatever will follow her last.

Bill strives, above all, to break records. With a fresh set of single-age and age-group records to challenge after each birthday, Bill need never run out of goals to keep him active and excited about competing.

Masters running should, first and foremost, promote participation. We should rate the success of an event by how many people run in how many different divisions, and not just by who runs fastest in their early forties.

Masters running should provide equality of competitive opportunity. It should recognize the toll that age takes on speed, and thus pit runners against only others their own age at the races and in the record books. It should give an 80-year-old's victory or record equal weight with a 40-year-old's.

Masters running should recognize that survival ultimately is our greatest and most lasting reward. Youth may fade, speed may decline, but training and racing can go on and on.

An "Olympics" for All

Competition for masters is still a young movement. With their 1989 running in Eugene, Oregon, the World Veterans Championships were only 14 years old.

Like a child of that age, masters running is both growing and maturing quickly. We're just beginning to see what its adult identity might be.

In its short life, running for this age-group has already produced three generations of winners. First came the new and renewed athletes. These people who hadn't competed since their youth, if then, started training for fitness as adults and couldn't stop with that. They created the first demand for separate veterans' meets, and won most of the early prizes.

This generation included Jim O'Neil and Dr. Alex Ratelle, who both remain active in their sixties. O'Neil, a Californian, rediscovered running at about 40 and has competed in every national and world meet. Ratelle, from Minnesota, ran for the first time at about 40 and much later broke 2:30 in the marathon.

The new opportunities for masters gave long-time runners in their thirties a new reason to continue. Soon, a second generation of winning masters was born—formerly near-great athletes who won by outlasting the people who had outrun them in their youth.

Hal Higdon of Indiana and Ray Hatton, a Briton transplanted to Oregon, best represent this generation. Neither made an Olympic team in their prime years, but both set masters records in their forties and fifties.

Now, the third generation is emerging. Superstars who remained competitive until they reached masters status include Kenyan miler Mike Boit, who won an Olympic medal at 23, and, of course, Bill Rodgers, who started his Boston and New York winning streaks in his twenties.

Women have evolved more slowly because they got a later start in this sport. But they've followed the same pattern.

Three American women personify the generational shifts: early winner Ruth Anderson, near-great Laurie Binder, and many-time Olympian Francie Larrieu Smith, who at 36 counted as a veteran under international rules and had planned to run in Eugene until an injury intruded.

For both sexes, the quality of competition has improved vastly. So has the quantity of competitors. The World Veterans Championships have more than tripled in size since the first edition at Toronto in 1975. But while growing bigger and better, the Championships haven't strayed from the original purpose: to serve the athletes, not the interests of nations or fans.

Contrast this approach with the management of older international meets for younger athletes. The Youth Worlds are limited to members of national teams (and no more than three athletes per country per event). Masters, on the other hand, enter their Worlds as individuals.

The Youth Worlds cater to spectators by limiting the size and number of races conducted. But the Vets Worlds make room for anyone who wants to compete, no matter how unwieldy the program grows. No one is turned away because of advanced age, lack of ability, or overcrowded fields. The meet just adds more age-groups and heats as demand warrants.

While reporting on the meet in Eugene, it was tempting to dwell on only a few athletes and events. But the medal-winners, record-setters, and superstars weren't the biggest story.

The top story was *all* the people who came to Oregon to compete—not to win, in most cases, but to do their best. This is a meet for getting out on the track, field, or road and pushing one's limits—not for sitting on the sidelines and worshipping the winners.

As the World Veterans Championships have grown, they've stayed truer to the original Olympic ideal than the Olympics have. The glory at the Vets Worlds isn't reserved for the athletes who place first, but extends to everyone who takes part.

"I truly enjoyed it," said Mr. Olympics himself, four-time discus winner Al Oerter. "This is what the Baron [de Coubertin] had in mind when he started the modern Olympic movement way back when. This is more like the Olympics than the Olympics. It's the spirit of participation."

Handicapping and Magic Numbers

George Sheehan, M.D., is a better runner in his seventies than he was in his teens. He has found a way to roll back the clock that says he should be slowing with age.

In 1989, Dr. Sheehan returned to "the race of my youth." He ran 800 meters at the World Veterans Championships, placing seventh in his age-group with 2:48.

Dr. Sheehan wrote then in a *Runner's World* column, "When I was flying home, I went through the tables that grade performances by age. How did my 2:48 compare with the half-miles I ran at Brooklyn Prep? A little calculation showed that my mark in Eugene was equivalent to breaking 2 minutes, something I could never do in high school."

To evaluate his performance, Dr. Sheehan used a statistical table developed by the World Association of Veteran Athletes and *National Masters News*, which revalues times according to the runner's age. Multiplying a time by an age-grading factor instantly cancels the penalties of aging. (See "Age-Graded Scoring" on pages 170 and 171.)

Dr. Sheehan's magic number for his 800 race was 0.7083, meaning the tables forgave about 30 percent of his time due to age. His mark then equaled a younger runner's 1:59.

Age-grading can relieve two problems in masters running: the inevitable and often depressing slowdown with age, and the confusion with age-group awards. These tables give runners a way to improve indefinitely, and they give race officials a way to award fewer but more meaningful prizes.

Let's look at the second problem first. When publications list masters winners, they usually mention only the leading men and women in their early forties. Older masters get too little credit.

But the opposite problem is true at the competition. Some masters get *too much* credit. The size of age-groups and the quality of their performances vary widely, yet most races give *all* groups the same number and type of prizes. This practice inflates the cost of a race and drags out its awards program.

Age-grading can streamline the awarding. *National Masters News* editor Al Sheahen writes,"In a track meet, medals can be awarded for each event rather than for each five-year age division in each event. In a road race, medals and recognition can go to the best performers, regardless of age."

Statistics exist for scoring open runners with masters and women with men in a single set of results. That pushes handicapping too far. We still need to reward overall leaders of each sex separately.

Races still can profit, both logistically and competitively, by reducing the masters groupings to two: men and women. A computer can factor in each person's age and spew out converted times in place order.

Top masters times become incredible under this system: Priscilla Welch's 2:26:51 marathon at age 42 converts to a world women's record of 2:17:46. John Campbell's 2:11:04 at 41 drops to a world best of 2:05:04. Marion Irvine's 40-minute 10-K at 59 is worth 31:43, a time few young American women have bettered. Norm Green's 33-minute time for a 10-K at 57 carries a value of 27:22, matching the world road mark.

But you don't have to be world-class, or even stand to win a local masters prize, to put the age-graded scoring tables to work. If you can read a chart and punch a calculator, you can roll back the penalties of the years.

BR Bill on the Future

You might think that the sheer number of competitors over the age of 40 would keep masters running growing and prospering for a long time to come. You could look to the seniors golf tour for inspiration.

Golf appeals to an older crowd. These recreational golfers now look up to such over-50 stars as Jack Nicklaus, Arnold Palmer, and Lee Trevino as their heroes. It's said that the crowds at seniors tournaments are larger that those at most of the events featuring the younger pros. The crowds love the old guys.

The same thing could happen in road racing. With the number of masters runners and their proportion of race fields growing all the time, the quality of masters competition and the number of big-name masters athletes should grow at the same rate.

But this won't happen automatically. It will require more promotional efforts.

Masters running is getting bigger and better, but not as quickly as I would hope. I place much of the blame on race directors. Many of them simply don't understand the positive impact that a high-quality field of over-40 athletes can have on their races.

Right now, there are too few stars in masters running. Priscilla Welch, Frank Shorter, John Campbell, and I are about the only names that people recognize.

Race directors need to work harder at recruiting and promoting the older heroes. For instance, four-time Olympic champion Lasse Viren from Finland and two-time gold medalist Waldemar Cierpinski from Germany both still compete, and both are masters.

It was good to see Campbell break the world masters marathon record at the 1990 Boston Marathon. But his feat would have had much more impact if he had gotten more publicity for running 2:11:04.

That spring, the national media were hailing the feats of 43-year-old baseball pitcher Nolan Ryan and several other athletes in their forties. They didn't mention John Campbell.

Part of the problem is Boston's lack of coverage on a major television
(continued on page 172)

Age-Graded Scoring

You can't make time stand still. But there is a way to adjust better to its passage and penalties.

Scoring tables from the World Association of Veteran Athletes (WAVA) and *National Masters News* serve two main purposes: (1) as a handicapping device for races to give older masters the chance to compete equally against younger ones, and (2) as a way to measure the relative worth of your own current times against those you ran at an earlier age.

Races using age-graded scoring must multiply each time by the four-digit factor listed below for the race's distance and the runner's age and sex. These calculations yield times adjusted to what they might have been if everyone had run in the open division (ages 34 and below).

Men			Age	Women		
Mile	5-K/25-K	Marathon		Mile	5-K/25-K	Marathon
0.9333	0.9430	0.9560	40	0.9266	0.9373	0.9516
0.9274	0.9370	0.9500	41	0.9201	0.9307	0.9450
0.9214	0.9310	0.9438	42	0.9135	0.9241	0.9382
0.9154	0.9249	0.9377	43	0.9069	0.9174	0.9314
0.9093	0.9187	0.9314	44	0.9002	0.9106	0.9245
0.9031	0.9125	0.9251	45	0.8934	0.9037	0.9176
0.8971	0.9064	0.9190	46	0.8868	0.8970	0.9109
0.8910	0.9002	0.9127	47	0.8800	0.8902	0.9039
0.8846	0.8938	0.9061	48	0.8731	0.8831	0.8968
0.8781	0.8872	0.8995	49	0.8659	0.8759	0.8894
0.8714	0.8804	0.8926	50	0.8585	0.8684	0.8819
0.8646	0.8735	0.8856	51	0.8510	0.8608	0.8742
0.8576	0.8664	0.8784	52	0.8433	0.8530	0.8663
0.8504	0.8591	0.8710	53	0.8354	0.8450	0.8582
0.8430	0.8517	0.8635	54	0.8273	0.8369	0.8499
0.8355	0.8441	0.8558	55	0.8190	0.8285	0.8414
0.8276	0.8362	0.8478	56	0.8104	0.8198	0.8326
0.8197	0.8282	0.8397	57	0.8017	0.8110	0.8237
0.8117	0.8201	0.8315	58	0.7929	0.8021	0.8147
0.8037	0.8120	0.8233	59	0.7841	0.7932	0.8056
0.7956	0.8038	0.8150	60	0.7752	0.7842	0.7965
0.7875	0.7956	0.8067	61	0.7663	0.7752	0.7874
0.7793	0.7874	0.7983	62	0.7572	0.7661	0.7782
0.7711	0.7790	0.7899	63	0.7482	0.7569	0.7689
0.7628	0.7706	0.7814	64	0.7390	0.7477	0.7595
0.7544	0.7622	0.7728	65	0.7298	0.7384	0.7501

You can do your own calculating to put your times in young-runner terms. Or, better yet, you can compare your present times to those you attained years before. Find your age, then the race distance and corresponding adjustment factor on the men's or women's side of the chart. Multiply your time by that factor (remembering to convert minutes and seconds to decimals).

For example, a 47-year-old woman runs a 10-K in 45:06. Her multiplier is 0.8902. The math is as follows: 45.1 × 0.8902 = 40.15, or an age-graded time of 40:09 (after converting the decimal into seconds).

National Masters News publishes the booklet *Masters Age-Graded Tables*, which includes scoring data for all events and complete instructions. For more information, write to Box 16597, North Hollywood, CA 91615.

| | **Men** | | **Age** | | **Women** | |
Mile	5-K/25-K	Marathon		Mile	5-K/25-K	Marathon
0.7460	0.7537	0.7641	66	0.7205	0.7290	0.7406
0.7375	0.7451	0.7554	67	0.7112	0.7196	0.7310
0.7290	0.7365	0.7467	68	0.7019	0.7101	0.7214
0.7205	0.7279	0.7380	69	0.6925	0.7006	0.7118
0.7119	0.7192	0.7292	70	0.6831	0.6911	0.7021
0.7033	0.7106	0.7204	71	0.6737	0.6816	0.6925
0.6947	0.7019	0.7116	72	0.6642	0.6721	0.6828
0.6861	0.6932	0.7028	73	0.6547	0.6625	0.6731
0.6775	0.6844	0.6940	74	0.6452	0.6529	0.6634
0.6688	0.6757	0.6851	75	0.6357	0.6433	0.6536
0.6602	0.6670	0.6763	76	0.6262	0.6337	0.6439
0.6515	0.6582	0.6674	77	0.6167	0.6241	0.6342
0.6429	0.6495	0.6585	78	0.6071	0.6144	0.6244
0.6341	0.6406	0.6496	79	0.5975	0.6047	0.6146
0.6254	0.6318	0.6406	80	0.5879	0.5950	0.6047
0.6166	0.6230	0.6316	81	0.5783	0.5853	0.5948
0.6079	0.6141	0.6226	82	0.5686	0.5755	0.5849
0.5991	0.6052	0.6136	83	0.5589	0.5657	0.5749
0.5902	0.5963	0.6045	84	0.5492	0.5559	0.5650
0.5814	0.5874	0.5955	85	0.5395	0.5461	0.5550
0.5726	0.5785	0.5865	86	0.5298	0.5363	0.5450
0.5637	0.5695	0.5774	87	0.5200	0.5264	0.5351
0.5549	0.5606	0.5684	88	0.5103	0.5166	0.5251
0.5460	0.5516	0.5593	89	0.5006	0.5068	0.5152
0.5372	0.5427	0.5503	90	0.4909	0.4970	0.5053

network. Would the Kentucky Derby be shown on some rinky-dink cable channel? Of course not, and yet the "Derby" of running is treated like some third-rate fishing tournament.

I don't mean to be totally negative. On the grass roots level, road racing is one of the strongest sports in the country.

Our sport reminds me of soccer, which also is very good for health and fitness, and has reached a high level of participation in the United States. Yet both sports have had a hard time taking the next step up in professionalism.

If masters running is to keep getting better as well as bigger, it needs more media exposure for the major events and the leading runners. It also needs long-term sponsorship, such as what John Hancock has given the Boston Marathon and what Mobil has supplied to the track and field circuit. You can't treat a great sport cheaply and expect it to prosper. ■

PW Priscilla on the Future

I haven't yet resigned myself to the fact that I'm a masters runner. I still think of myself as an open runner and try my best to keep up with the open girls.

My goal since turning 40 in 1984 hasn't been to win the masters division of races or to set world age-group records. I've been able to win most of the time and set some masters records without making this my focus.

But my thinking will have to change. The time is coming when I'll have to take masters competition very seriously. I've gotten away with murder up until now in the masters division, but I'll soon become vulnerable in these races.

Some extremely talented women are approaching 40. Carla Beurskens of the Netherlands, who will become a master in early 1992, has run a 2:26 marathon and in the low-32s for a 10-K. Francie Larrieu Smith has made four U.S. Olympic teams at distances from 1500 to 10,000 meters and will try for another in the marathon in 1992, shortly before her 40th birthday. The legendary Grete Waitz of Norway, who has lowered the world marathon record numerous times and has run the 10-K in 31 minutes flat, will reach 40 in 1993.

It will do me good to have these women come up. I'll be 48 by then and may be hard pressed to compete with them, but I'll welcome them as masters. Our races will be as exciting for me as the open events have always been.

Lots of other women are racing well in their mid- to late thirties. How well they'll continue to run as masters depends on how successful they are at avoiding injuries.

Holding together is the real problem when you get on in age. You can still produce the results if you get to the starting line, but staying healthy in between the races is the difficult part.

As long as I can hold together, I'll keep racing. I'm prepared to feel vulnerable, because it will make me hungrier. I'll work as hard as ever to win but won't stop trying if I lose.

As I tell other masters women, the thrill of racing isn't winning all the time. It's participating the best you can. ■

You, Too, Can Be a Champ

Do you dream of running in international competition? Well, your dream can come true if you're a master and can pay your own way to the meet.

The World Association of Veteran Athletes (WAVA) has conducted World Veterans Championships every odd-numbered year since 1975. (World Championships for younger athletes didn't begin until 1983.) Turku, Finland, is the site for the 1991 games.

The championships award three medals in each event for every age-group, but also emphasize participation. There are no qualifying standards and no limits on the size of events. Runners may enter any number of races.

The only qualification is age. Competition is divided into five-year groupings and starts at 40 for men and 35 for women.

These championships include all of the Olympic running events, 100 meters through marathon, plus some that the Games don't have. Masters women run the 5000 meters and steeplechase, and both sexes compete in 10-K cross-country and 10-K road races.

The championships are held all over the world. Since its start in 1975 in Toronto, Canada, other sites have included Sweden, West Germany, New Zealand, Puerto Rico, Italy, and Australia. The 1989 championships were held in Eugene, Oregon. Tokyo is the favorite for the 1993 championship games.

The Athletics Congress (TAC) conducts similar U.S. National Masters Track Championships each year, but holds its annual road and cross-country races separately. While the track meet has enjoyed autonomy and continuity, the off-track distance races often blend into open events and in some years aren't held at all.

The track nationals began informally in 1968 and became official championships in 1971. TAC's title events usually contain submasters categories 30 to 34 and 35 to 39 for both men and women. And just like WAVA, there are no qualifications or limitations whatsoever. Anyone can enter as many events as he or she likes.

Finish Lines

Work on this book began in mid-1989. We'd barely started writing when Ed Ayres, editor of *Running Times* magazine, asked me to break away from this manuscript long enough to consider the future.

"As we prepare to enter the new decade — the last of the millennium — I am inviting a small group of people to write about what they envision for the sport in the next decade," Ayres said in a letter. I told him I'd already seen a preview of running's future and was eager to see more. In that future, the world grows smaller and friendlier, and age loses many of its old burdens.

Ayres asked his contributors to write in terms of "here's what will be. . . ." I told him what already had happened at the World Veterans Championships in my hometown of Eugene, Oregon, that summer.

My neighborhood track happens to be the most famous one in the country. Anyone can run at Hayward Field on the University of Oregon campus, and I often drop by to see who's there.

This July day, the noontime crowd looked the same as always but sounded quite different than ever before. As usual, runners of diverse ages and skills lapped the track at their own paces and for their own reasons.

But now, one group spoke Swedish. A couple talked in German, another Italian, another French. Words of British-, Australian-, and New Zealand-accented English floated across the track.

Three Finns finished their workouts and joined me for lunch. We talked about the things that runners everywhere always discuss.

The world had come to visit Eugene. I'd known for almost two years that the Vets Championships would be here that summer. But it was one thing to read that 5,000 athletes from 58 countries would be coming, and quite another to see and hear them arrive for a two-week stay.

These first looks at them and talks with them moved me more than I thought possible. I was filled with pride in Eugene for bringing this event home, and with runner-pride in knowing that the sport means so many of the same things to so many people in so many different languages.

These runners weren't typical tourists. "They weren't here just to take part in the events and enjoy a vacation. They came to *compete*," said meet director Tom Jordan. "Even I was surprised."

Business was slower than expected at the city's finer restaurants. Same with the hotels and motels. The competitors weren't looking for luxury. They were looking for convenience.

Legendary master, author, and physician Dr. George Sheehan could have afforded to dine and sleep at the city's finest. Instead, he chose a dorm room (without phone, TV, or private bath) and took his meals in a dining hall (self-serve, self-cleanup). With Hayward Field conveniently nearby, thousands of others made the same choice.

Dr. Sheehan spoke during the games on why we run. "It provides us with a setting for contemplation, conversation, and competition," he said. He could have added another value that these visitors demonstrated: concentration on what they came here to do.

As the competitors marched in the opening ceremonies, my companion called them "the elite of the planet." These vets aren't elite because they run, but are runners because they're elite. They have worked hard enough, stayed healthy enough, become prosperous enough, and been lucky enough to come this far in both age and distance.

Another running author, Hal Higdon, then 58 and a racer since his teens, competed in Eugene. He wrote later, "I concluded that what I was witnessing was not eternal youth but rather the art of survival.

"Those of us who continue to excel as masters do not necessarily demonstrate more skill or determination than others. We've simply learned better to avoid the twin problems of injury and indifference that cause so many others to drop early from competition."

Eugene-based sports psychologist Dr. Scott Pengelly said during this meet that "90 percent of winning is showing up." Wanting to reach the starting line is most of the battle.

The most exciting prospect for the rest of the 1990s and on into the next millennium? Growing numbers of runners learning how to beat those twin demons of injury and indifference that conspire to end the race of a lifetime before it really starts. A race that really begins in the masters years.

Joe Henderson

Index

Page references in **boldface** indicate tables.